Divorce is
Self-Defeat

Divorce is Self-Defeat

Enid Muragira

authorHOUSE®

AuthorHouse™ UK Ltd.
1663 Liberty Drive
Bloomington, IN 47403 USA
www.authorhouse.co.uk
Phone: 0800.197.4150

Published by AuthorHouse   05/07/2013

ISBN: 978-1-4817-9479-4 (sc)
ISBN: 978-1-4817-9480-0 (hc)
ISBN: 978-1-4817-9481-7 (e)

About the Book

The principles in this book demonstrate how one can embrace roles and faith to sustain a happy marriage. It provides guidelines for how these roles can be implemented to help achieve our God-given tasks.

The challenges we encounter should not make us give up on our motives; rather, they should strengthen us to grow in understanding. Our faith should make us understand the purpose of living, helping us to be more reliant on what we believe. If you are going through a horrible experience, it should give you the zeal to see a better tomorrow when you have not lost what you stand for.

The book demonstrates how faith should be embraced with appropriate actions. It holds both physical and spiritual principles that, when applied, act as antibiotics to domestic violence and vaccination for divorce and emotional and physical abuse to children. Although there is often a focus on a person's rights in society, ignoring the roles and responsibilities of each person would be an error.

Contents

Part A. Introduction 1
   i.   The Purpose of this Book 5
   ii. Stop Being Selfish 7
   iii. Let the Will of God Manifest in You....................... 10

Part B. Keys to Sustain a Marriage................................ 12
   i.   Have a Positive Perspective................................... 12
   ii. Have Plans and Determination to Achieve Your Dream 14
   iii. Develop and Answer Questions for Yourself............... 16

Part C. Christian Marriage and the Value That Jesus Christ
        Adds to Your Marriage Life 21
   i.   Jesus Is a Miracle Worker 24
   ii. Jesus Is a Healer 25
   iii. Jesus Knows Everything 27

Part D. Prayer and Works... 29
   i.   Prayer 29
   ii. Works 31

Part E. Aspire for the Best Results 34
   i.   Try Accepting Your Spouse the Way He or She Is............ 34
   ii. Even Unfaithfulness Can Be Managed 37
   iii. Learn to Give Your Spouse's Needs Priority............. 42
   iv. Identify Each Other's Roles................................. 44
   v. Be Submissive 48
   vi. Learn to Exercise Your Goodness 50
   vii. Enjoy Being a Mother and Wife 56
   viii. Practice Wisdom with Your Feminine Power............ 59

Part F. Value Transformation...................................... 68
   i.   Your Appearance 68
   ii. Activities 68
   iii. Mind Your Language 71
   iv. Clothing 73

v.   Making Requests 73
vi. Treat Anger with Wisdom 79
vii. Giving Advice 85

Part G. Conclusion **91**

Foreword

Uwimana Enid writes an eye-opening book that can strengthen any marriage for the glory of God. *Divorce Is Self-Defeat* provides valuable points that will lead readers on the right path for a successful marriage. It not only gives in-depth information about the role of husbands and wives within marriage but also gives practical advice that is bound to bring a positive, prosperous change.

We all know that many are capable of sustaining a marriage, but can people keep their partners happy, respected, and loved the way they need? If you are asking yourself these questions, *Divorce Is Self-Defeat* is the answer.

This book will cause you to get out of your comfort zone and stare your weaknesses in the face.

You will be able to recognize the problems in your marriage, apply the solutions in this book to strengthen your marriage, and create an unbreakable bond between you, God, and your spouse. All around the world, today's society has made divorce common. However, God did not create man to be alone and certainly did not design marriage covenants to be ruined by divorce. In fact, as the title states, divorce is self-defeat. This book will help you put the enemy under your feet and take back your marriage and its intended purpose, according to God's plan. This book is bound to inspire and impact readers worldwide.

Dr Apostle Paul Gitwaza

Endorsements

The almighty God designed and created human life. He is the source of all knowledge and understanding of a good marriage. The marriage is a godly project, planned before men and women were created. It is a blood covenant that no one is admitted to break once it has been entered it. This is why every marriage led by God's principles is supposed to be successful. Divorce is not allowed for any reason. Jesus responded to the Pharisees in Mathew 19 regarding divorce, saying that the only reason for a divorce was the unfaithfulness of one of the partners, but He emphasized that it was not so from the beginning but only because of their hardheartedness. He was essentially saying that there is no reason for a marriage to be broken apart.

History has proven that the majority of divorced people live in greater misery than when they lived together with their spouse. The "pharmacy" for treating divorce, provided in this book, instructs us—among other medicines—to get wisdom from God. Research shows that a good marriage is not attained through knowledge acquired at school but rather from knowledge acquired through praying, meditating on the Bible, and putting biblical principles into practice. Then, you will be able to treat each other with love, submission, perseverance, respect, consideration, positivity, protection, and honour and to always live with regard to your relationship with Christ.

The devil hates marriage because he knows that married couples will:

- Live a life of joy and happiness
- Be blessed
- Overcome evil
- Develop and impact the world
- Transform the earth

Divorce Is Self-Defeat is not only a book but a living testimony of the author and a guide for all of us to live better within our marriages. This book is a must, and it will help you overcome temptations and intrigues of the enemy and be able to save your marriage. You can and you will make it, 'Not by might nor by power, but by my Spirit, Zechariah 4:6.

May God use this book to transform millions of marriages, in Jesus's name.

Revd Vuningoma Dieudonne

Endorsement by the Author's Husband

I thank my beloved wife for the wonderful message in this book, *Divorce is Self-Defeat*. I strongly believe that whoever reads this book will not remain the same. Thank you again for your courage and initiative to share this wise message. I would say it's a book for this generation. It will strengthen the married couples and prepare young people for the future. With a happy marriage, life becomes more meaningful.

Eric Mutabaruka

Acknowledgements

I give all the glory to the Lord Jesus who loves me so much and protected me till the day He opened my eyes to see the truth of his will and tell this good news to the world. And because he is able, may he protect me and find me telling this truth until the day He decides that I should go to live with him. I can't imagine the world without you in my heart, Lord. I only know it would be much different and a much less comforting place.

Next, I thank all the good servants of God's work, who shone the light of true salvation into my life. I had been to many churches, but the experience at Zion Temple Celebration Centre is different. No other name befits you but home. Dear servants of the Lord, thank you from the bottom of my heart for your commitment to feed us with what is in the heart of our creator. I value you and consider you parents and dear friends.

Relatives and friends, you are so many that I surely could not list you all out on paper. To those I am bonded with by blood relationship, those with whom I share beliefs, workmates, schoolmates, or who I've met in any other walk of life: The things you do for me do not go unnoticed. You're a necessary part of my writing this book. I appreciate your presence in my life, and may God bless you.

To my parents, Frank and Norah Muragira, and my husband's parents, Mrs Bernadette and the late Elijah Mutabaruka (Mbamba), I only wish to aspire to the things you've taught me. Telling you that you're appreciated does not do you enough justice. You're the best!

I thank Eric, my husband, who did not get bored of talking about this book every day. I will always cherish your encouragement to complete what I started. I thank Blair and Bill for your ideas. You appear so young but had input for this book; that's wonderful. Thanks, Ketsia and Bruce, for always giving us courage to smile by asking so many questions when you needed attention. No words can express, no act of gratitude can relay, and no gift can represent what your love and support have meant to me. You deserve to be called co-writers. May God be with you always.

PART A.

Introduction

"The words of a man's mouth are deep waters[1]" Let this message spread beyond what human imagination might expect, to the young and old, especially those who find their lives feeling like a sinking boat. I bring a message of relief: no matter where you are, the sea can be still again. Jesus's profession is to restore life's dignity!

At the end of a day Jesus told His disciples[2], "Come with Me. We will cross to the other side." It was His only chance of getting away from the crowds. At first the water was calm. It only seemed like a few moments later when they felt the boat nearly go over. They must be caught in the middle of a storm. All at once, they felt afraid. The wind kept changing. They were able to grab onto the side. This kept them from being swept overboard by the huge waves. Waves broke over both sides of the boat at once. Men scurried back and forth. The boat tilted madly from one side to the other. These men felt helpless. They looked at each other, and remembered "We have to get Jesus!" When they saw Him asleep, they woke Jesus up. "Teacher! The sea is wild. This is a terrible storm! Save us!" Jesus looked from one troubled face to the other, and then He got up. Jesus spread His arms wide. The wind blew hair into His face. His voice boomed, "Be still!" As soon as Jesus called out, "Quiet! Be still!" the wind calmed. The water flattened.

I use the story of a sinking boat to try to bring the message from my heart to any reader with a marriage that has lost meaning. Perhaps you don't see a way through the challenges, and you feel you have reached a dead end. To begin to find an answer, it is important to act right and

---

Notes:
[1]   Proverbs 18:4 ESV
[2]   Luke 8:22-25 NAS

1

have faith, hope, and confidence that God, your creator, knows where you are and is aware of what you are going through. Marriage is a journey decided by our creator, the God who never fails, on the creation of the universe, among other things, He created woman from a man's rib, offered her to the man and decided, *"For this reason a man will leave his father and mother and be united to his wife, and they will become one flesh"³*. He does not ignore you, but He wants to manifest himself in you. There are strengths He put in you that can only be exposed by crossing a wild sea through a terrible storm. You are not an imposter; that marriage is yours by the virtue of who you are, no matter what. But just like in the sinking boat story above, Jesus Christ has identified you, but He cannot give you the assignment from this side. He wants you to cross the sea to the other side. Perhaps Jesus has observed that your character and your attitude need to mature so that you reach your divine destiny as a wife, a mother, and a homemaker. There are twelve important things you need to understand from the story about crossing the sea, as they relate to your life.

1. You have a calling. Always remember who called you, especially before you take the next stride and the winds blow.
2. Every day has its own tests; pay attention to even the small choices you make.
3. You are not alone in the struggle. There are others on the boat, even though the task of crossing is your own.
4. Jesus is right there with you in the boat. He is not scared or bothered by the surrounding noise. However terrible the storm may be, he is peaceful because he is the Prince of Peace. He does not want to force Himself into your life but is ready to intervene when you call on Him.
5. Jesus wants to give you another identity and special clothing, but this is earned. You cannot cheat; you must pass every other test to earn this reward.
6. No one can cross the sea for you, because it is your character and attitude that Jesus wants to transform.

Notes:
³   Mathew 19:5 NIV

7. In your worries, you still have a voice to shout and awaken Him! The disciples said, "The sea is wild. This is a terrible storm! Save us!" The wild sea reflects unfair circumstances. Do not quit; shout to Jesus, for he knows that sometimes our faith is not enough to contain the fear caused by the terrible storm and the wild sea. He is merciful; he cares for and is able to save you.
8. Whatever is bothering you will obey his voice and be still.
9. It is amazing when the battle is over and the situation is calm.
10. Life is good when you stand in your territory with victory.
11. Be mindful of your destiny.
12. Make a choice to leave a legacy of confidence in your children.

I pray for courage to those who are determined and for strength—that this message will lift up those who are bent down in depression. You are beautiful, amazingly created, and talented. You're highly treasured by God, and a bright future is just in front of you. Let these life-giving words break the chains of depression; let the chains of low self-esteem be broken. May you be set free from the strongholds that make you feel fed up with your circumstances. May God use His strength and power to begin and continue the healing process and to bring every person reading these words into a brand new lifestyle.

The title of this book comes from the inner feelings experienced after the storm, when the sea is still and all the noise is gone. Now that the sunrise has brought a bright day, I look around and see that no one around me was left behind. On a new day with another blessing, I said, "surely divorce is self-defeat." No wonder God says in Malachi 2: 16, "I hate divorce."

We encounter a number of challenges in our everyday lives; due to sickness, poverty, rejection, opposition, and so forth; the list is long. We overcome some of these problems with ease and others with much difficulty. However, in all circumstances, when hopes are threatened to the point that even life may be lost, we need not to fear. Whether circumstances are good or bad, there is always noise. In a good environment, the noise is because of rejoicing; when people eat and dance, there is noise. In the same way, where there are problems, there is the noise of people running away in terror. When our projects are being threatened, we should not be scared; that is just the noise of the army fighting. Even if the noise is coming from you rather than other people, just tell yourself that it will not fool you. Be strengthened by one thing, you cannot be a failure when you have Jesus the Saviour.

When a child is born, parents have a lot of expectations of what that child will be when he or she grows up. But since God knew us before our parents, He said things about our lives before our parents or anybody else, and these things must come to pass. What your parents say may never pass because they are only people, and they have many limitations. In contrast, what God speaks has power to fight limitations; its force is overwhelming. For example, God had declared that Elijah would never die on earth but ascend to heaven while alive. However, one day Elijah was threatened. He had destroyed the altars of Baal and killed the false prophets, and everyone in Israel shouted in worship of Elijah and his God, but then Jezebel scared him, and Elijah ran away to the forest and asked God to allow his death (see 1 Kings 18-19). Similarly, your presence in your home may be scaring the devil, but perhaps you do not know that, and you want to run away. Remember: what God planned in your life must come to pass; just stand strong.

Is pride in worldly possessions enticing you not to yield to possessing the virtues of a wife? Consider the biblical story of a man named Naaman, a Syrian, found in 2 Kings 5. He was a soldier whose honour and great valour had earned him the position of "captain of the host of the king of Syria, 2 Kings. 5: 1". But Naaman was a leper. Leprosy is a bacterial disease that attacks the nerves in a person's hands, feet, and face. It horribly disfigures its victims. After Naaman found out that Elisha could heal the disease, he went to see him, but Elisha did not come out to pay tribute to this important man of Syria. When Elisha sent a messenger to tell Naaman to dip himself seven times in the river of Jordan, Naaman felt disrespected and decided to go back, but his men advised him to try it, probably because they loved him so much. When Naaman dipped himself in the river, his skin became healed and clean, like that of a baby. Surely Naaman was sick, but he was also proud; maybe he had reason to be proud, but he clung to his pride even though it almost prevented him from being healed. Imagine that you are like Naaman in your status today; I call it being fooled. Pride about what we are or what we own may lead us into a great loss of focus, simply because we fail to understand what is important. In other words, what is important should be related to your destiny, not circumstances. Why should we cling to honour, status, and pride when they haven't given us peace? The pursuit of these things may even be making us loose our health. As noted previously, leprosy attacks the nerves, and it discolours the victim's skin; he or she is totally deformed and becomes a different person. In the same way, when you lose your divine identity, you become a different person, to the extent that you might even reject yourself.

The people who were with Naaman saw that his leprosy was destroying him but he was proud, so they reasoned with him, saying, *"Sir, if the prophet had told you to do something very difficult, wouldn't you have done it? So you should certainly obey him when he says simply, 'Go and wash and be cured*[4]*!* Naaman was not cured of his leprosy by the method he expected. He was only cured after he had done all that he had been asked to do. The purpose of this book, similarly, is to give you wisdom and remind you that the keys to total happiness and a meaningful life involve taking the sour pills of perseverance. It's high time we understand that if we are not happy in our homes or families, this is the "leprosy" we must deal with. Just like Naaman, we cannot be saved by what we think or feel is the right thing to do, no matter how sincere we may be. We can only be saved according to the plan God has laid out for us in His word. Drop the pride and save your marriage, my friend. Save your husband or wife from feeling ashamed of having chosen you as a spouse; save your children from the consequences and do not leave room for regret. One divorced friend confessed to me, "Sad to say, I have moved out and in the process of getting divorce—I must say, it does make one feel like a failure."

i.   *The Purpose of this Book*

This book contains antibiotics for domestic violence and vaccination for divorce and emotional or physical abuse. If you pay attention to the

---

Notes:

[4]   2 Kings 5:13 NLT

5

information and practice the recommendations appropriately, it will change your mind-set, not only in marriage but in your life as a whole.

This book provides basic guidelines to those intending to join the institution of marriage or those who are already married. When you read it and do exactly as it says, not only will you see your home changing for the better but also you will be completely transformed and renewed in spirit. Let me put it clearly: when you are sick, you need to see a doctor who specializes in your type of sickness. For example, you cannot run to the ophthalmologist (eye doctor) when you are pregnant; in the same way, when you have a problem with relationships in your home, you need to rush to the specialist in these matters. That is none other than Jesus Christ, the one who is able to tell the wind and the storm to be still. Separation and divorce will not satisfy you; instead, they will take you away from your calling and make you feel like your existence is a mistake.

There are effects that come along with separation and divorce that will make you feel unwanted in society. Don't allow yourself room for regret. Perhaps we think of getting a divorce because we have lost inner happiness. However, inner happiness is a quality of spirit which must be earned by a victory over our weaknesses and an upward reach for perfection of our character. It is found in great efforts and achievement of life and in faithful devotion to duty.

Inner happiness is seated in the heart, and it consists of things like serenity, tranquillity, peace, faith, and a sweet, calm spirit that spreads over one's face and then into his or her actions. It is among the angelic traits and is a worthy character required in a wife, mother, and homemaker. You know you have inner happiness when you can weather life's storms with a calm and peaceful spirit. It doesn't mean you won't have problems, but the way you handle them will portray whether you understand this peaceful attitude; lack of it is viewed as a deficiency. Inner happiness enables us to spread joy around and cast light upon dark days. Unhappiness is caused by a defect of character, failure to meet responsibilities, or being the centre of your own universe.

On the other hand, we set the stage for happiness to grow when we overcome our defects of character, fulfil responsibilities, serve others instead of ourselves, and live according to heavenly laws. Happiness is not caused by good surroundings or having everything just right. We can be surrounded by things that please us and still have unhappy hearts. There is nothing wrong with these possessions or amenities, but they don't bring happiness. Inner happiness comes from following the spiritual laws concerning happiness. In addition to the material here, there a few, important principles that can bring women inner happiness found in the book Fascinating Womanhood, which has saved many marriages. Success in your home will bring you inner happiness. This is the first area that you must succeed in, in the roles of compassionate wife, diligent mother, and successful keeper of the home. The key to your happiness lies within your own hands. Achieving this goal may require you to go beyond what you expected, but it's worth it.

ii.   Stop Being Selfish

When you are in a situation that is so uncomfortable that even others do not feel good about it, the solution is not to run away from it but to find solutions to make it a better place. It is an opportunity for you to demonstrate values that can change the situation and bring peace. Hiding, giving unfavourable excuses, or running away from such a situation is ignoring your responsibility and failure, hence, selfishness. Truly happy people have a high moral character. They are usually honest, dependable, giving, loving, kind, not easily angered, thoughtful, and unselfish. You can easily observe these types of traits. Following eternal laws leads to happiness; following a path of sin leads to unhappiness. No one could say following these commands is an easy option, but it's a road that leads somewhere good. Choose to serve others; considering the option of divorce is brought about by selfishness. Don't let your life become nullified by focusing only on yourself and your individual dreams. Someone may be as dirty as crude oil on his or her own merit, but when refined, he or she would be turned into a wonderful person, as desirable as petrol all it requires is patience, understanding, and acceptance of undergoing the refinery process.

It helps to accept yourself and what has happened to you; allowing yourself to make errors will help you be happy with yourself and enable you accept the errors of others. Don't let the discouragement you might feel from past failures or mistakes defeat your efforts to grow or steal your blessings. Take time to think about yourself and appreciate every little thing in life, even the simplest things that did not last long. The Apostle Paul had this trait; he said he was able to be content in whatever state he was in, and he was in some horrible circumstances. He was able to be happy in feast or famine, among turmoil, and amidst poverty or wealth. Cultivate inner peace rather than finding contentment in your surroundings.

Look around at society and try to understand that you are not alone in your needs. Knowledge is the key to unlock the door of happiness, and wisdom provides the power to open it. This search for wisdom and knowledge should be the highest priority of our daily lives. You need to know what to do and how to do it. You also need to know what to avoid and how to avoid it. If you don't know how to build your character, it may be difficult to be happy wherever you go.

Many people make the mistake of placing the blame on others, taking all the credit and heaping blame on the circumstances. These people make excuses in their own favour because they believe they are always correct and in order. For example, "If only he [or she] loved me, then I would be happy or I would not have done this . . ." Having the love of your spouse or any other person is essential to attaining inner happiness, but you must work hard to achieve it. Inner happiness has nothing to do with the feelings of another person. When you have inner happiness and your husband doesn't love you, there will be something missing from your life. But as you cultivate and practice goodness, this goodness tills the soil that his love can grow in. The key to your happiness lies within yourself and not in your surroundings.

Family law, especially the portion concerning divorce, exists because people continue to ignore the principles of marriage designed by Him who formed the institution of marriage. Some of the lawyers facilitating in divorce cases understand the emotional roller coaster that divorcing spouses can experience. "Divorce can be a confusing and emotionally a painful event"[5]. However, it is high time people understand that the challenges of marriage are a spiritual war and not one fought with physical weapons, such as a cannon. Marriage should be guarded spiritually by the people involved, and each member of the couple should appropriately exercise their roles at home, in order to avoid the sad experience of divorce. "For Jesus is the one referred to in the Scriptures, where it says, *"the stone you builders rejected, which has become the cornerstone"*[6]. Divorce has become the option for many, but I suppose if one opted to sacrifice happiness for the moment, there is an alternative that would empower you to overcome the dangers that have led others to sign a divorce certificate. When Jesus came to earth, He did not come to rescue angels, but mankind. *"For surely it is not angels he helps, but Abraham's descendants"*[7]. You became the descendant of Abraham when you received Jesus Christ as your Lord and Saviour, and even if you haven't yet, there is still a chance for you to accept Him and do his will. For those who have accepted Jesus, you are a child of God who should grow up and claim your inheritance. *"See how very much our Father loves us, for he calls us his children, and that is what we are! But the people who belong to this world don't recognize that we are God's children because they don't know him"*[8]. Being married is our inheritance, whereas signing a divorce certificate is like giving away our heritage. Now that you know who you are, therefore, do his will; his rewards are extraordinary and eternal. The sacrifice you are required to make is for your calling here on earth and also for you to receive a special place in heaven. This does not mean that you are to die as a sacrifice here on earth; not at all. The Lord will manifest in you here on earth because his miracle-working power is for use on the earth. We will not need miracles in heaven. Stand strong; he stands with you the whole way.

Notes:

[5] htt://www.voitfamilylaw.com/, Attorney Catherine H. Voit

[6] Acts 4:11NIV

[7] Hebrews 2:16 NIV

[8] 1st John 3:1 NLT

iii. Let the Will of God Manifest in You

God and the devil both operate from one's home. The institution of marriage was established by God for Adam to have a companion and be happy. But the devil comes to destroy the good that God wants there to exist in a marriage. If you don't understand this, women will keep running from man to man, or men run from woman to woman, yet every person was created for the same purpose. Those who understand this secret do not run away when challenges show up; their interest is to have a marriage that is sustained and enjoyable. Couples do not get married by mistake; God gave us all the tools in this arena so that He may be manifested in us. People around the world need to know God; when we stand strong in our callings, He will be manifested by His works in us. This is a task from God, and we shall give account for the responsibility we were given. This task will be achieved by women who have discovered their destiny and purpose in life and who are committed to changing the world for the positive by accepting a role of being tools for our Lord. *"Like clay in the hand of the potter, so are you in my hand"*[9] says the Lord. The goal of this book is to help you look beyond your challenges in the struggle you may be undergoing; it focuses on personal understanding and self-empowerment so that the will of God may be manifested. I believe that God did not make a mistake when He said, *"I hate divorce" (Mal. 2: 16)*. He hates divorce because He has given us all the tools in order to prevent failure. He is aware that the journey is not smooth, not a bed of roses; He is with us along the way. *"Have I not commanded you? Be strong and courageous. Do not be afraid; do not be discouraged, for the LORD your God will be with you wherever you go"*[10].

There are challenges and setbacks to this road, but you can overcome them all once you know the principles of personal understanding and self-empowerment that will help you achieve your destiny and purpose in life. I encourage you with the seven blessings God gives to those who love Him. Our love is manifested by our level of sacrificial dependence

Notes:
[9]   Jeremiah 8:16 NIV
[10] Joshua 1:9 NIV

on Him. *"He who dwells in the shelter of the Most High will abide in the shadow of the Almighty . . ."*[11].

One might ask, why all that sacrifice and all that pain. If we are to be happy, then we must accept God moulding us into a vessel with a shape that He likes; He alone knows the tasks he has designed us for. And it is all for the best, for he says, *"For I know the plans I have for you," declares the Lord, "plans to prosper you and not to harm you, plans to give you hope and a future"*[12]. It is so amazing, but only those who have accepted being moulded by God can testify to this. I am personally among them, and I tell you out of my own testimony: it is so amazing. God is true to His word, and His salvation is so full of life.

Psalms 91: 14-16 says, "'Because he loves me,' says the Lord":

1. I will rescue him;
2. I will protect him, for he acknowledges my name.
3. He will call upon me, and I will answer him;
4. I will be with him in trouble,
5. I will deliver him and honour him.
6. With long life will I satisfy him and
7. Show him my salvation.

Let go of all other options and chose God's way. He will help you forget all the pain and sorrow that you went through. Trust in His word; it is real. *"The LORD your God is in your midst, a mighty one who will save"*[13].

Notes:

[11] Psalms 91:1 ESV

[12] Jeremiah 29:11 NIV

[13] Zephaniah 3:17 ESV

PART B.

Keys to Sustain a Marriage

i.   *Have a Positive Perspective*

Marriage is a gift from God. That's why the devil is always at war to steal this precious gift. As married women, we should understand that no matter where the man came from—what he's been through, who he knows, and in whatever way he may know that person—you are blessed in the eyes of God and that man. Just like Adam did, he saw you and said, *"This at last, is bone of my bones and flesh of my flesh . . ."*[14]. This should give every married woman the strength and courage to move on, no matter what she may be facing in her marriage. You are the one who your husband chose to take before the Lord God, amidst relatives and friends, and you both said, "Till death do us part." Marriage is a treasure that you have to guard with all the strength you have. Paul puts it, *"Guard what has been entrusted to you. Avoid the pointless discussions and contradictions of what is falsely called knowledge"*[15]. As a wife, homemaker, and a mother, your marriage is entrusted to you, and the rest follows. When we women stand before our Lord, I am sure He will greet us of us with: "How are you, daughter?" The next question will be, "How is he?" (your husband). "How are they?" (your kids), and then the rest will follow. Let us fight well. *"But you, man of God, flee from all this, and pursue righteousness, godliness, faith, love, endurance and gentleness. Fight the good fight of the faith. Take hold of the eternal life to which you were called when you made your good confession in the presence of many witnesses. In the sight of God, who gives life to everything, and of Christ Jesus, who while testifying before Pontius Pilate made the good confession, I charge you to keep this command without spot or blame until the appearing of our Lord*

Notes:
[14]   Genesis 2:23ESV
[15]   1st Timothy 6:20 NIV

Jesus Christ, which God will bring about in his own time—God, the blessed and only Ruler, the King of kings and Lord of lords, who alone is immortal and who lives in unapproachable light, whom no one has seen or can see. To him be honor and might forever. Amen"[16].

This is why we are interested in having a marriage that is sustained and enjoyable until we take a report to our heavenly Father. This is why God created women; He gave us all the tools we needed and gave us the arena of marriage. It is our mission, and we will be asked to give account on how we exercised our rights as women of God. Just as Jesus Christ came, lived on earth, carried out his mission, and took back the report, and we should do the same.

There are thousands of known and unknown reasons men and women have experienced challenges in marriage, in the past and in the present. Many of these couples are not and never will be well-known individuals, but they have become weary and fallen into the hands of the enemy known as divorce. Maybe we should feel sorry for them; the dangers of divorce still exist, and you will find them everywhere: in every country, profession, race, culture, and religion. But for those of us who can focus on what God desires, let's pick up our tools and fight. He who says He hates divorce also says, *"Do not be afraid or discouraged because of this vast army [of challenges]. For the battle is not yours, but God's"*[17]. He is telling revealing what is before us. Sister, why should we lose heart? Let's guard our posts; there is a great reward when we reach our heavenly home. After all, God gives us courage to live as queens, *"What shall we say about such wonderful things as these? If God is for us, who can ever be against us"*[18]?

However, we can never live as queens without understanding ourselves and focusing on fulfilling our roles with self-empowerment. Some individuals believe that one person can make a difference in the world,

---

Notes:

[16]   1st Timothy 6:11-16 NIV

[17]   2 Chronicles 20:15 NIV

[18]   Romans 8:31 NLT

and that together, we can take humanity and the planet, including marriage, to the next level of potential. These are women who have discovered their destiny and purpose in life, so that they can maintain their marriage, sustain themselves, and say no to the power of divorce or anything else that would want to push them away from their post.

Those who are married and those who want to get married need to focus their mind set on this set of principles because, in addition to passion, we need marriage tools. More importantly, we need a solid inner foundation of knowing who we are, why we are here, and what marriage is all about. In other words, we need to become conscious and authentically believe in God's desires. Just like any other profession or business, marriage also has norms and principles that when not complied with, no matter what, a marriage relationship will fail or become hell on earth. A lot can be said about the union of men and women, but we desire to talk about personal understanding and self-empowerment. These things can help a woman (wife, homemaker, and mother) achieve her destiny and purpose in life.

ii. *Have Plans and Determination to Achieve Your Dream*

Almost everyone daydreams about getting married, having children, and other things they want for the future; but we forget that in order to reap these good things, we must sow and carry out all the activities up to the reaping stage. All too often, the exercise ends as a daydream We need to have a vision of how our homes should look like, this will help us discover our destiny and purpose in life and then make a plan to get there.

The reality is that most of us never stop to think about how we will get from point A to point B, that is, from where we are to where we want to be. We fail to identify who we are now, and worse still, we have no plan in place to achieve the successful marriage that we dreamt about. That is a huge problem, and it's the reason why when anything goes wrong, we resort to false solutions, including divorce. A woman needs to develop a foundation for a successful marriage, get a clear understanding of where she is going, and then make a plan to get there. Otherwise, she will find herself wandering aimlessly around the battlefields of marriage, eventually quitting or living a miserable life. There are some things about relationships we can never change, such as the following statement by God: "*. . . And your desire shall be to your husband, and he shall rule over you*"[19]. My dear sister, let's not be proud; it's not about your background, level of education, beauty, age, size, or height with your husband, who will satisfy your desires.

When you first set out to be married, you need to have some ideas about what it will look like when you get there. But you cannot figure out exactly what it will look like without knowing the players, and you cannot know the nature and character of both sides; therefore, the best strategy is to concentrate on your side and leave the other side to God, for "*Nothing in all creation is hidden from God's sight, everything is uncovered and laid bare before the eye of him to whom we must give account*"[20]. Sometimes the human nature is selfish; it tends to concentrate on what it will receive without giving much attention to what it can offer. Again, it is hard to know what to offer before knowing what you are offering, why you are offering it, and to whom you should offer it. Personal understanding will give you the answers to these questions in your vision or dream; but until you have that dream, you are like someone on a military mission without a clear understanding of success, and you wind up with a futile and dangerous exercise.

Marriage is a life and in life there are challenges, some challenges in life are beyond imagination, and sometimes you find yourself being pushed to the edge. But when you know the almighty God is there, you do not need to be afraid. God, your creator, loves you and will never forsake you; even in a dark corner, his hand can reach to save you. You may need to bend, but God will save your marriage. "*No temptation has overtaken you that is not common to man. God is faithful, and he will not let you be tempted beyond your ability, but with the temptation he will also provide the way of escape, that you may be able to endure it.*"[21]. When you know who you are and you are sure that you have someone who loves you, also

Notes:

[19]   Genesis 3:16 AKJV

[20]   Hebrews 4:13 NIV

[21]   1ˢᵗ Corinthians 10:13 ESV

be sure that God is there and has allowed you to pass through testing because he has confidence that you can make it. Then ask God, "Father, what do you want me to learn from these circumstances?" Be patient, and you will definitely get an answer. Be positive; every challenge is a test, whether you seem to have caused it or it dropped on you. The way you respond to that test is what is important because it will determine your failure or victory in life. Don't be deceived, my sister or brother; divorce is never the best choice.

iii. Develop and Answer Questions for Yourself

Gaining personal understanding is part of the solution for a number of problems we find ourselves in. This will help you understand the kind of person you are and what you stand for, and then you can overcome the challenges around you. There are five principles that would help everyone establish a solid foundation for life, no matter the circumstances. These principles can help in business operations, profit or non-profit-making, and in marriages. They can be applied naturally in all circumstances, but the best results will be achieved if they are implemented with positivity. Whenever you try to solve a problem and you have a bias, you are already filling yourself with a wrong attitude, but when you do something with good intentions something good will definitely come out of it.

1. **The Why**—It is important to understand why you are where you are in your relationship. If necessary, go to an isolated place, like a park, or lock yourself in a room, and ask yourself why you are where you are. If you find no answer, think back and try to figure out how you arrived at this point. Surely you were not insane when you agreed to be there. You have not been in that relationship for only a day or two, how did you manage to stay there for more than a month? There must be some reason; give it a chance to yield some good results and keep thinking. If there are any good memories, even if just for a moment, they can be a seed to begin a foundation of something better.

   Unfortunately, when most people are challenged, they get bitter instead of wanting to learn from the challenges. Decide to pick out lessons from your challenges, and know that life is introducing you to different spheres of life. When you decide that, everything will not be bitter but rather interesting and exciting. Not everything bad is intended to hurt us, but some of them are lessons to help us grow up. You may not be able to avoid getting hurt, but you can decide not to get annoyed and instead replace your anger with asking why.

In addition, ask why you are going through the experience that is bothering you. This will guide you to examine yourself without disclosing your secrets to anyone; nowadays, confidants are hard to find. Be true to yourself; don't ignore anything, no matter how small it is. Try to establish who the beneficiaries of your success will be if things get better. Of course, as a mother, other people should come before you (priorities should be Jesus, others, and you last). That's the way I see it, as a Christian, and even those with different doctrines, please consider your children, who did not ask for their existence in this world. Judge your success in terms of the welfare of your family. For whom or for what purpose do you want to get or stay married? In other words, what is the purpose of your marriage? Be honest with yourself. If you dream of getting a divorce, understand the reasons behind this, and then work to make it real. But if your dream is to have a happy marriage, then understand its purpose and work to make it real. As a Christian, I have the word of God as my guide; I don't intend to say that I am perfect and holy, but I understand that for Jesus Christ to save us sinners, who received unmerited grace, Jesus understood why he had come. One of the reasons wasto die for us and so that we may get divine Grace. He knew what would be the fate of mankind if He did not accept to die. He died a terrible death, killed by those he was dying for, who didn't believe in Him. It was a tense moment for the King of kings, *"Going a little farther, he fell with his face to the ground and prayed, "My Father, if it is possible, may this cup be taken from me. Yet not as I will, but as you will"*[22]. In the same way, accepting to persist in an abusive relationship is another tense moment, I am refusing to say it's like Jesus at Gethsemane just for the respect I feel for the Lord

---

Notes:

[22] Matthew 26:39 NIV

but it is another hard decision. No one should take you for granted. I have gone through it and understand clearly what it means, but after deciding on the why, I made up my mind, and that is how I know we can make it. I stand with you, my sister and brother, to support you with words of courage and love; we can excel in marriage and help the next generation.

2. **Have Courage**—I mention courage here because I know that in certain situations, fear is present. Fear isn't a sign of failure or of weakness. In fact, going through challenges without at least some sense of fear shows foolishness or stupidity. You and your loved ones need to respect the magnitude of what you're facing but not to be distracted by it. Being paralyzed by fear is something else. And courage is the tool you need in order to tear down your fear. Stand firm, and always remember, when the waves of challenges threaten you, someone is lifting you up, and that's why your heart hasn't stopped pumping. Consider each new day a blessing, and develop courage to wait a little longer; every day that passes draws you closer to the end of the struggle. As you develop courage, the one who lifts you today will do so to the end. Don't think or dream of leaving your home or separating your kids from their father. Instead, develop the courage to push on and wait for your blessing. Developing courage also allows you to do whatever it takes in order to achieve your destiny and purpose in life. It is your cross to carry. Don't lose hope; instead, take heart. The journey with this cross is for a short time, like a day, but the crown you're rewarded with will be forever. The experience you acquire while being courageous will give you happiness—not only for you but also for your loved ones. In relationship challenges, just like in any other struggle, it takes courage to move forward and win. The more you learn to proceed, especially when you're afraid, the more successful you'll be in your life.

3. **Knowledge Is Necessary**—Knowing your enemy is very important, and in most cases, enemies are invisible. You might be fighting or putting the blame on the wrong person; this is a mistake. The person you can see might not be the one waging war against you. Focusing on the person you perceive as the enemy limits the scope of your battle. This is a weakness. Every person has three great enemies: the devil, the world, and the flesh. All three of these operate in your life,

and each has agents to work against you. But until you understand these three enemies and the way they operate against you, you will fight hard and loose. You therefore need to be knowledgeable about your enemies and the best way to approach them as well as knowing your weapons. *"Be sober-minded; be watchful. Your adversary the devil prowls around like a roaring lion, seeking someone to devour. Resist him, firm in your faith, knowing that the same kinds of suffering are being experienced by your brotherhood throughout the world"*[23].

Your most powerful enemy is the flesh, part of yourself which sometimes dictates to you. Depending on the circumstances, you may think it is right. It shows you dangers before they come and scares you with death and shows you many other options. After you have obeyed your flesh, it keeps quiet and leaves you with no solutions, overwhelmed with circumstances and regrets. It is the voice that whispers to you, suggesting divorce before knowledge exercises its power. In every area of life, knowledge is power, whether it's an understanding of who the enemy is or what the enemy is doing at a given time. Knowledge is the key to help you understand where to focus your fight. If Eve had known that her family was being attacked by the devil, I doubt she would have even touched the fruit from the forbidden tree. Ignorance can cause a lot of damage, not only in marriage but in life. Endeavour to have knowledge—it is power! The Bible says, *"and give no opportunity to the devil"*[24]; otherwise, ignorance opens the gates to defeat. The more you know about how marriage can be attacked and should be protected, the more skills you acquire and the more successful will be at achieving your purpose in life as a wife, homemaker, and mother. And the more you understand about your role and implement these skills in an appropriate manner, the more success you'll experience. Keep learning; it is a lifelong process. Nothing bad comes from knowing more, especially if your enemies encroach upon your destiny in life.

Notes:
[23] 1st Peter 5:8-14 ESV
[24] Ephesians 4:27 ESV

4. **The Will**—Your will is your fuel; it gives you zeal and strengthens your courage. Having the will to make your marriage work regardless of the circumstances is an anointing. Your will is nothing more than the determination to win. I also believe that it represents discipline—the ability to see a task through to completion regardless of what it takes. In other words, your will enhances your resoluteness to do things that you might not necessarily enjoy but that are part of accomplishing your mission and achieving your purpose in life. A strong will enables you to put forth the maximum effort necessary to win. In the Bible[25], a person called Zacchaeus was a chief tax collector and a wealthy man who made up his mind one day to see Jesus, and he decided to climb a tree, not caring about his status; he did not give up as he faced the problem of his height. None of the people closely surrounding Jesus hosted him that day, but Zacchaeus did. Jesus knows why we go to Him. Just like He saw the zeal in Zacchaeus's heart, He can see your heart and come into your life.

5. **Setting Priorities**—Prioritizing keeps you firmly focused on your why. Knowing what's most important and focusing on those critical elements is also an essential aspect of achieving success. You will run into a lot of potential distractions on your road to success, especially when things are not going well in your marriage. It is important to understand your calling in life. Pick your battles wisely. Evaluate each opportunity carefully to make sure it fits well with your overall objectives. Setting priorities isn't a casual pursuit. Spend the necessary time to evaluate all that is in front of you before you make any decision. Jesus came to save all of mankind, but here on earth, He identified who His calling focused on. He said, *"I was sent only to the lost sheep of the house of Israel . . . . It is not right to take the children's bread and throw it to the dogs"*[26]. Our time here is just for a short while; we cannot involve ourselves in everything that comes our way and think we will remain focused. Your calling, too, has its time; embrace it and use divine weapons as you pursue it.

Notes:
[25] Luke 19:1-10 ESV
[26] Mathew 15: 24 & 26 ESV

PART C.

Christian Marriage and the Value That Jesus Christ Adds to Your Marriage Life

---

Marriage

I am not going to say much about the origin of marriage, because various cultures have different theories on the origin of marriage. However, according to the Bible, marriage is a divine institution because it was instituted by God Himself. The first person to bless a wedding was God, when he made Adam sleep and created Eve out of his rib, and both lived in the garden of Eden. He has now delegated this power to pastors—His ambassadors—to bless those who show interest in living together as a married couple. God gave them His word for couples to abide by if they want to be happily married. Those who drop out of this state of happiness are violating the norms of the institution, and there are no two ways about it: either drop out or live a satisfying life. *"Marriage should be honored by all, and the marriage bed kept pure, for God will judge the adulterer and all the sexually immoral"*[27].

Times have driven some individuals away from getting married for so many reasons which are best known to them. For the majority, it is probably out of frustration because of what they have heard, experienced, or imagined about troubled married couples, but that does not remove the importance of getting married. It is important that one gets married because God, who loves humankind, saw that it is not good for a man be alone. He needs a helper similar to him, and God created a woman

---

Notes:
[27]   Hebrews 13:4 NIV

so that they may live together, be happy, and enjoy the pleasures of this world.

It is also important for people to get married because through marriage, the human race procreates. Unless a man and woman get married and they bear children together, the human race may cease to exit.

Another reason it is important to get married is because two are better than one. For this world to be a better place to live in, one needs company; even those who own pets are looking for company, so why not instead build a relationship with a fellow human being, with whom you are easily compatible.

Getting married satisfies the biological, physiological, and psychological needs of humans. For example, one time in the Bible, hunger struck the land, and Isaac went to a foreign land. He told the people in the land that Rebekah was his sister, not his wife, but one day the king saw Isaac showing Rebekah more than sisterly affection. *"Abimelech [king of the Philistines] called Isaac and said, 'Behold, certainly she is your wife"*[28]*!* This demonstrates how it is sometimes very difficult to hold back feelings for your spouse.

It is therefore important that if two people are committed and to each other and are convinced that they wish to live together, a pastor should join them in marriage and be their mentor until they are both mature believers. It would be best for them to get saved before they are married, but since this is not always possible, it may be done after the couple has gotten married.

Marriage vows are promises that each partner in a couple makes to the other during their wedding ceremony. There is no wedding where these vows are not made. Some couples develop their own vows, and others read the traditional ones before their pastor, parents, relatives, and friends. As one repeats these marriage vows, it seems like he or she is

---

Notes:
[28]   Genesis 26:19 NASB

very confident, but after a short period, the confidence is gone for some people.

Traditional Marriage Vows

The following vows were adopted from a local church.

For couples who get married in the church, the man and woman essentially make the same pledge to one another. According to the rite of marriage, the customary text in English is:

> I, ____, take you, ____, to be my [husband/wife]. I promise to be true to you in good times and in bad, in sickness and in health. I will love you and honour you all the days of my life.

Or

> I, ____, take you, ____, to be my lawfully wedded[husband/ wife], to have and to hold, from this day forward, for better, for worse, for richer, for poorer, in sickness and in health, until death do us part.

"The priest will then say aloud 'You have declared your consent before the church. May the Lord, in His goodness, strengthen your consent and fill you both with his blessings. That what God has joined, men must not divide. Amen."

I wish every couple would repeat these vows to each other every morning before they step out of their bedroom; I am sure the benefit of doing this would be reflected in their daily lives. Unfortunately, most couples recite them from the altar and leave them there. When they meet challenges in their marriages, they forget that the priest blessed them with the Lord's goodness, strength, and inseparable bond. People who were married in the church can get their bond to each other repaired; do not just give up and opt for divorce. Go back the Lord who joined you; He still loves you. He longs to save your marriage, and He is able to do so.

The Value That Jesus Christ Adds to Your Marriage Life

When you have Jesus Christ in your heart, not only do you live a sinless life that is pleasing to the Lord. You also accommodate to a number of elements more easily than if Jesus Christ were not living in you. Remember, He says you can do nothing without Him. For example, the challenges that couples encounter may have solutions based on using other people's experiences or your own wisdom and understanding, but these options may not be godly. They may instead drive you away from your divine purpose as a wife, mother, and homemaker. This is exactly what the devil wants you to opt for. He causes a problem and shows you exactly what you could do to get rid of that problem, when in fact that choice would worsen the situation. However, amidst the challenges, you may not understand the consequences of the alternative suggested from a source other than God. When you are already in the middle of the dilemma, the facts show up, and you may regret a choice for the rest of your life.

When you are in Christ Jesus, you will be prepared for what to expect. Jesus will inform you in advance, and if you pray, He gives you wisdom for how to overcome challenges. Even when He tells you and you do not understand him, Jesus brings wise people (His true servants) to help you overcome those problems. Whether you are happy or sad He never leaves you alone, because He knows the devil can use both to take your soul. The value of having Jesus Christ in your marriage is that you will always be victorious.

i.   *Jesus Is a Miracle Worker*

Jesus restores the dead back to life. If you believe this and allow Him to work in you, He can restore all that was dead inside you and around you, starting immediately. Consider the biblical story of Lazarus, who was dead and buried; when Jesus arrived, mourning stopped because Jesus resurrected Lazarus[29]. I am sure that Martha and Mary, the sisters of the

---

Notes:

[29] John 11:1-44 NASB

dead man, could not believe it at first because they had never heard of resurrection. But you and I are lucky; we have heard of it several times. All we need is faith that Jesus is able to do such a thing. In addition to Lazarus, Jesus performed many life-restoring miracles. No matter the severity of the death of your circumstances, life can be restored to them. There are people alive now who can testify to this, including those whose marriages were dead, lacking happiness, love, care, and sensitivity. These relationships were hellishly miserable, but with faith in the Lord and by doing what was required, the relationships were restored, and the couples are happily married again. The birth of this book is another miracle that came out of a challenging situation.

ii. *Jesus Is a Healer*

I once heard a pastor say that if circumstances are horrible, we should consider them to be a sickness. That imagery works. When you see your spouse's weaknesses as a disease, you become sympathetic, and that puts you in a position of wanting to serve him or her. Then it will be easy to make sacrifices out of the love you have for that person as you try your best to see a better person returning. In a way these weaknesses really are a sickness; at the time the two of you got married, your spouse wasn't like that. Therefore, consider these problems attacks that need to be treated, and with Jesus they will surely get healed. I don't know how long you or your spouse have been weak, but there was a sick man who lived by the water for thirty-eight years[30], too sick and weak to get up and dip himself in the waters with healing power. He was sick, but he expected to get support from other sick people who had come to the well to get cured. Of course, if they weren't sick they would have been somewhere else, doing productive work and planning for the future, not sitting at the well. In the same way, if someone, including your spouse, was better off than you, he or she would be helpful; but because you are both sick, neither individual has time for the other. When someone is sick and not being helped, he or she blames those nearby. This is exactly what most married couples do when their marriage is failing—they blame others

Notes:

[30] John 5: 1-16 NASB

for their failures. Jesus's healing of the man at the well demonstrates that rather than blaming others, we need to find Jesus and ask for His help.

Maybe you don't know that you are sick because there are forces that have filled your mind with a different understanding. This commonly happens, and it is unfortunate when both of you are sick (i.e., if you both have weaknesses that can lead to a failed marriage) because neither one of you will help the other. In this case, you may need a wise friend who knows the truth and can guide you toward helping yourselves. After reading this chapter, go to church and hear the truth being taught. You will experience the healing power of Jesus; anything harmful that stole your understanding will be destroyed, and you will know what to do and when to do it. When Jesus met the man who was infested with a legion of demons, they flew away from him, and he was set free. God's healing power knows what your worries are, and He is ready to heal you.

In the Bible[31], when Jesus took a long time to reach Jairus and heal his daughter, people got distraught because Jesus was not rushing, even though Jairus had told Him that the daughter was sick and dying. Jesus said, "Don't be afraid. If you will only believe, the little girl will be well." All Jairus had to do was to believe. When he did this, Jesus went to the man's home and laid hands on the little girl, and she came back to life. I don't know what type of sickness (weakness) you have or how long you have lived with it; it could be doubt, lust, greed, denial, opposition, anger, you name it. But if you believe that Jesus Christ heals and seek Him, all will be well.

When it comes to accusing others, married couples often take the lead; they are very good at it. Thank God they are not allowed to give the final verdict. Also, thank God for sending His son, Jesus Christ, who has all the mercy, grace, and joy that we need. When the woman who had been caught in adultery was brought to Jesus, He bent down and wrote, "*Let any one of you who is without sin be the first to throw a stone*

Notes:

[31] Luke 8:40-56 NASB

at her"[32]. Everyone who read this disappeared, and when the woman and Jesus were alone, He said to her, in effect, "You are forgiven, but don't do it again." Maybe you are being harassed with accusations for something you did. This is because you haven't met Jesus yet. Just as it happened for the woman in this story, all will flee, and when you are alone with Jesus, you will receive the mercy, grace, and joy that you need, and you will see your accusers no more.

iii. Jesus Knows Everything

In another story from the Bible,[33] the Samaritan woman could not believe what she heard when Jesus, a man she had just met at the village well, could expose all her secrets. He is aware of everything in our lives, even the things that were done in the dark, behind closed doors, or behind bars. Confess your sins and struggles to Him, for He cares for his sheep.

It is important to understand that Jesus can never violate the choices we make. He says, *"Look! I stand at the door and knock. If you hear my voice and open the door, I will come in, and we will share a meal together as friends"*[34]. Jesus respects our personal space; He knows we were given the right to choice by our Father, and He will not just break down the door. For Jesus to act in one's life, a person needs to do his or her part make a choice according to His will, not yours. He comes to you like a VIP (*very important person*); He knows and respects the place you give Him in your life. He is so patient with you, and when you give Him an appropriate seat in your heart, He never rests. That's when you start growing from one level to another, day by day, and the fruit of the Spirit will manifest in you. If you only put him in your eyes, remember that sometimes they fall asleep; if He is in your ears, remember that sometimes you are far away and disconnected. If you put Him in your arms or legs, remember that sometimes you will not to do anything or go anywhere. That that's

---

Notes:

[32] John 8:7 NIV

[33] John 4: 3-42 NASB

[34] Revelations 3:20 NLT

why I choose the heart; it never fails to pump so long as you are still exposed to the devil, the flesh, and the systems of this world. Jesus understands when it is His turn to act, and you will see your miracles; you will receive your healing because he knows everything.

PART D.

Prayer and Works

i. Prayer

It is hard to go through life without praying. Prayer is a necessity in every area of life. Even those that don't pray—if these people exist—make a wish, and that wish is their prayer. I should have made prayer the first point on the list of principles, but it's not very rewarding to pray until you identify why you are praying and what you are praying for. However, after going through all these steps, it's possible you now understand that you need to build a good marriage, but you cannot achieve your objectives by your own strength. When you understand this, humble yourself and seek God's intervention. At this stage, you can be sure of your request before the Lord; you must pray every day, again and again, with faith and determination. God loves right intentions; He is happy with those who carry out His desires, and He will definitely intervene in the situation.

Many marriages are challenged, even those of Christians who believe in the power of the Holy Spirit. These challenges do not need an invitation to enter your home; they do not fear anybody—the newly married, the middle-aged, and even the elderly have been challenged. Neither do the challenges in marriage fear the profession a couple has excelled in or feel sorry for uneducated couples; these problems do not fear intercessors or consider the respect people give you in public. The challenges marriages can face are not deterred by the rank on your shoulder or the great family that you come from; even dynasties have been challenged. They invade any territory all you have to demonstrate is to show that you love and fear God.

Women (the wives, home makers, and mothers), you hold the keys for our marriages to be sustained and happy or to keep out every blessing that God prepared for the man who married you. There are those who go to church, worship God, give their tithes and offerings, shout halleluiah, and even persuade their husbands to come and watch them pray at home or in church, but sometimes that does not bring them towards their calling as wives, homemakers, or mothers—towards their destiny in life. Some women are aware of this problem but do not want to give up their pride, whereas others are ignorant of who they are and what they should do. To those who do not believe in the Bible, you need to vanity apply the principles of being a good wife, homemaker, and mother. I don't have much faith in the possibility of doing this without the strength and inspiration given by the unfailing helper, the Holy Spirit. But practice them whatever the case; God knows you and loves you where you are, and He has a plan for you.

But for my dear fellow Christian women, we have a helper, who Jesus promised to his disciples when he ascended to heaven: the Holy Spirit. He never fails, and He walks with us to the end. However, we need to sincerely respond to His invitation, His guidelines, and His principles. *"Can two people walk together without agreeing on the direction?"*[35]? We need to allow the Spirit of the Lord to take us his way instead of whatever else we think we can rely on; we must allow ourselves to be guided by He who can drive better. Some of us still cling to our vanity, which does not count for much. If we do this, we shall pray over and over but fail to get the answer. *"Truly, truly, I say to you, unless a grain of wheat falls into the earth and dies, it remains alone; but if it dies, it bears much fruit"*[36]. Maybe what you are clinging to is worthless, and you think about yourself too much. (For example: I am still young and pretty, my father loved me, I am learned, with a masters, Ph.D, I hold a powerful post, I earn more than my partner, I have my rights.) Ladies, think of all valueless excuses you can make. All these and more will not overrule your desires, and there is no middle ground; it's yes or no. You will not have your desires satisfied unless you are cherished by your husband. You will divorce him and get another man, but until you know who you should be and you have the will and courage to stand at your post, you will still

---

Notes:
[35]   Amos 3:3 NLT
[36]   John 12:24 ESV

lose and end up becoming an outcast in society. However, with prayer and these simple principles, you can save and sustain your marriage and live happily "till death do you part."

ii. Works

When I talk of works, I don't mean the job you do; I mean the role of a woman at home. In the twenty-first century, women have become breadwinners and enjoyed having large bank accounts, expensive cars, and personal belongings. All this is good and nice to look at, but it is worthless when you are bringing up thugs—hostile and mannerless creatures—as the next generation. It is important to know that however hard-working you may be, if you put no value in your home, all your efforts are a waste. You are living like a flower which will wither, and its story is gone forever, and that reveals nothing but selfishness in you. A life that is not selfish sacrifices its life for others. Even when you are worn out from breadwinning, you can still go an extra mile with a happy heart to see what your family members need to survive.

Your good financial abilities are blessings from God to help you reach another status level. This is good and welcome; however, if you are not careful, this could cause misunderstanding. It is unfortunate that when some women get to this level, they forget the purpose of the blessing and want to use it to disregard their husbands, as if all they wanted was enough money to live a single life; very few men can stand being overlooked. Some ladies have forgotten their roles as women and mothers because they are contributing to breadwinning in the house. Even if you bring in the biggest share of earnings in the house or if you are the sole breadwinner, you still have to do your duty. Having a job does not change your role in the home as a mother, homemaker, and wife into something else.

Learn to have a good system of money management in your home; otherwise, if both the husband and wife are earning and do not manage finances very well, it can become another cause for misunderstanding in your marriage and you will likely waste your resources. You might want to have, for example, three different accounts where both spouses' earnings are collected and plan how all of your earnings are distributed.

There should be an account for everyday spending, and this may be managed by the one who has enough time to shop and who is not extravagant, after the two of you have agreed on how you will handle necessary expenses. There should be two savings accounts: one for your capital expenditures and the other for your children's education, if applicable. Every amount of extra income that you receive should accumulate in the capital savings account; perhaps when this account accumulates a large enough sum, you can then decide how to spend your savings on things that will generate income and or keep on reinvesting it. This kind of system for money management has a number of benefits; for example, it creates trust and confidence for you, and it will make your bankers trust you for an increased loan. This, in turn, can help you acquire more wealth and economic strength. Good money management will help you to maintain focus, plan schedules, and protect you from unnecessary outings and expenses; in most cases, these are the loopholes for mistresses. Mistresses typically prey on people who are careless. If you as the husband and wife manage money well, this will also help you train your kids about how to manage their finances when they grow up. Even when your spouse is weak and goes out extravagantly, you cannot be shaken if you have these principles of managing money in your life.

Worse still, there are some women who are fed, dressed, housed, and spoon-fed but have no virtues to contribute peace to the home or carry out the expected responsibilities of a mother, wife, and homemaker. These women are stubborn and nagging. They do not appreciate anything; all they say is, "This is not enough." They make their husbands steal to satisfy them, and they despise everything because they do not understand the pain and hardship others go through to get things done; they are the best time keepers, complaining when their spouse comes home late. If you are this person, I feel sorry for your spouse.

You need to do something—and do it right—in order to achieve what you want, the way you want it. Drop your pride and vanity and act; there are people, specifically your children, waiting for you to act rightly so they may enjoy their life. If you are a sensible person, you will have time for your family, organize the home, keep it smart, and pay attention to what people in your home eat and drink. Don't neglect to arrange everything, plan for events, and be positive no matter the circumstances.

For anything you don't understand, ask God for wisdom to make your home a happy environment for those who live there and visit. No matter what, if you maintain it, God will bless you and your family. Otherwise, your lack of character has denied them happiness, and you are bringing up hostile creatures as part of the next generation. There is a time for everything; praying about these things does not mean to turn church into your escape route every time. What you are required to do will wait for you. *"For just as the body without the spirit is dead, so faith without actions is also dead."*[37]. God will not send angels to do what He gave you the ability to by yourself. Regardless of the circumstances, act rightly, be positive, and let your intentions be godly. Having an approach of tit for tat isn't fair; instead, pay good for evil and forgive quickly, focusing on what is ahead.

Notes:

[37] James 2:26 ISV

PART E.

Aspire for the Best Results

There are secrets every married person should know; those who know and apply them have enjoyable relationships. I believe that practicing these things, together with prayer, can help us carry out our tasks easily and efficiently.

i. Try Accepting Your Spouse the Way He or She Is

Many marriages start out in ignorance, but when love is ahead, whether these people have passed through the formal procedure of marriage or not, they love each other intimately. There may be some important issues they did not address before marriage, but the main thing that unites people in marriage was there: love. This sort of couple forgets to discuss issues like character, finances, childbearing, and so on; at a later stage, when they find it is worth having the discussion, many address it through a viewpoint learned from experience in other relationships. For example, a man might expect his wife to be like his mother, sister, aunt, or any woman he knew before, and the woman might expect the man to treat her like her father, brother, uncle, or any man she knew. This creates confusion and dissatisfaction, because no person is like another; the problem may be even more severe if your partner does not know the person you want him or her to be like or that you have these expectations. These two people love each other very much, but they need advice on how to be patient, accept each other, and improve their communication. The couple must have great patience to understand each other; they must accept the process of learning and changing to adjust to suit each other's desires; two people cannot move in the same direction when they are in disagreement.

A grownup relationship requires understanding, acceptance and patience. Women, it is not right to compare your husband with others or to think you can change him to be like your father, brothers, uncles, boss, pastor, neighbours, or even your ex-boyfriends. Look at him; there must be something good that you are ignoring—remember the good things that made you fall for him at the beginning of the relationship. Consider those good traits and pray for his weaknesses and failures. When God brought Eve to Adam[38], she was presented as a helper, supporter, and companion. Maybe if Adam was not weak and did not need support or company, God would not have created Eve to live with him. God saw that Adam needed a companion, helper, and supporter to encourage him every day; if it had been only once in a while, perhaps God would have done it Himself. After all He used to visit Adam regularly.

And if I may talk to you, brother: you could not manage life alone. That's why God got you a suitable helper. However, you are forgetting some of the important roles expected of you. That is why your wife is frustrated and there's no peace at home. The most important role is for you to love her the way she wants; you prefer to love her in your own way. You never take time to understand what she likes and doesn't like, and she may not feel like you appreciate her. Love is demonstrated by actions; putting it into words should accompany those actions; unfortunately, some are even too shy to say they love their wives but do manage to be critical. This is so sad.

For both husband and wife: think about what you normally criticize, and stop it. Ask for forgiveness after you have prayed about it, and your spouse will forgive you. Sometimes we tell each other how others treated us well, even if it was not actually any better; when this happens, our spouse may feel offended. We probably said this because it's what or how we want him or her to treat us, but we are not confident to openly tell our loved ones that this is exactly what we want. It is best to say the way you feel, demonstrate it confidently and with love, and request that your partner try to understand. Your request may be granted, and even if not, you will have genuinely done your part.

Notes:

[38] Genesis 2:18 NASB

Showing great appreciation for others in front of your spouse, especially for something you want and your spouse has never done it or given it to you is rude. I do not mean appreciating others is bad, but you must be aware of what you are saying and why you are saying it. Even if it was something a family member did for you, when you tell your spouse, he or she could easily feel offended and take it to heart; this generates coldness in how he or she feels about you, which is a problem when your relationship becomes monotonous and unloving actions start between the two of you. I would advise you to accept your spouse no matter what and plan the healing process for your spouse. Maybe God will use you to transform him or her into a better person! This means accepting everything in him or her, good or bad. If you are so unlucky to have picked someone with poor character, then you will have to pray without ceasing until the Holy Spirit turns him or her into someone loving and caring; otherwise, when you give up on your spouse, it's a defeat in itself.

In the Old Testament[39], when Abigail was told that her husband, Nabal, had refused to assist David, she thought of a plan which saved the whole family. David was making plans to destroy everything that belonged to Nabal because he had refused to give food to David's men when they needed it. Despite Nabal's foolishness and drunkenness, Abigail defended the interests of her home; this is what every married person should consider when his or her spouse turns out to be different than expected.

There are many problems that can lead to families disintegrating, but for now, let me focus on finances. We are used to the traditional idea that men are breadwinners, but times have changed, and there are circumstances where women earn more than men. If one or both members of the couple don't practice acceptance, understanding, and patience in this situation, then your earnings may lead to a break-up of your marriage. Understand that being blessed with bigger earnings is a blessing which can be diverted at any time, and your spouse should share in this blessing. Manage your finances the way they should be used rather than letting your earnings manage the way you lead your life.

Notes:

[39] 1st Samuel 25:1-35 NASB

For those wives who earn little or nothing, please have a great deal of acceptance, understanding, and patience and appreciate what you get; earning a living is tiring. I cannot understand why you, a grown human being, decide to sit and be fed and cared for like a baby, but if that is what the two of you agreed upon, it is all right, and there should not be any complaints about finances. Alas, as much as every woman should expect to get financial support from her husband, she should also accept learning to live within his means. If he cannot afford something, live like it never existed and give him peace. Some husbands have become corrupt because they want to provide for the requests their nagging wives present to them repeatedly; in the man's desire to please his wife, he steals and gets caught and goes to jail. What shame we have brought to society. Ask God to give you the capacity and wisdom to live within your husband's means. If we were to be assessed on our responsibilities, we would realize we are not perfect; it's better to accept that others can sometimes fail to fulfil their responsibilities too. Accept everything and pray about what you feel is not right for you; there is no limit to how accepting you can be.

ii. *Even Unfaithfulness Can Be Managed*

By God's grace, some of us have been brought up with spiritual values and are told that sexual immorality is a bad thing before man and God. Even those from these backgrounds who sneak out and practice sexual immorality do so knowing they are committing sin punishable by human law and God's law. However, the blessing of considering sexual immorality unacceptable is not common to all cultures; there are those whose cultures do not instruct that sexual immorality is a sin; instead, it is treasured by people exchanging gifts after engaging in it. One friend of mine confessed how her sister-in-law came to her home to seek a cow as a gift because her husband's brother had had sexual relations with her, implying that when her husband comes, the brother's wife had to do it with him as well. In short, it's a culture where two brothers share wives in exchange for cows. In these cultures, they are very ignorant about what God says in Leviticus 18: 6-19. Such people have no respect for other people or for themselves; the lustful spirit inside them makes them have sex with several partners without fear or respect.

Therefore, before one gets married, it is important to know the cultural beliefs of your potential spouse before swimming in that pool. And if by chance or mistake you are already there and your culture is different, decide to be the saviour of that family and light your candle in the darkness. When you do not sleep with any of your spouse's siblings, some will feel jealous and hate you to death, but as time goes by, the light of your candle will glow, and they will one day appreciate your character.

Unfortunately, because we are ignorant about other people's culture, we sometimes accuse them of infidelity without considering their background, culture, and doctrines. Like they say, one man's meat is another man's poison. What you might look at as sin might be considered a blessing to another, and when you accuse him or her, you look ridiculous because it seems like you are depriving that person of his or her rights. For example, with people whose parents were polygamous and their fathers had ten wives each, if you start talking of infidelity, you would be considered the criminal or unusual person. To some people, living with only one man or woman is bizarre they have been told that God created one man for each woman but it's like it does not concern them. I think most humans need to be transformed to understand that God did this because He wants a generation that honours Him. This polygamous mind-set, just like any other unhealthy one, needs to be dealt with. A person with this view needs to be told that what he or she has believed for a lifetime is wrong, and this conversation and the following change takes a lot, including patience, great understanding, and acceptance. Some people have used King David and King Solomon as excuses to satisfy their selfish and lustful desires, but God is clear in His word and His nature.

When God was designing the family structure, there was no confusion about what He intended. It is important to note that even after Eve had distorted God' plan, He did not replace her with another woman, even though He was capable of doing this. Therefore, some people need to know the truth before they are accused of sexual immorality. Those who allow their bodies to be treated like doormats are living with false beliefs, and they need your support since you know the truth of how people should behave.

When someone is unfaithful, this is very disappointing. When there is infidelity in a marriage, it's possibly a result of ungodly homes being infested by demons, either in this person's past or the past of the person who tempts him or her. I have advice for you: live like you are blind to this and don't think of what goes on in that world. Put your sight and your heart into waiting for what God will do for you. He alone can change a man or woman to feel disgusted with having sex outside marriage. Your nagging won't change his or her heart. Even if you try doing what your spouse did, I doubt you would find a high level of satisfaction. Remember, your spouse had sex with someone because they admired each other, they felt feelings for each other, and then they chose to have sex; but if you are just doing it for revenge purposes, you would not get the same level of pleasure. Instead, you may end up a miserable man or woman, both physically and morally, frustrated and embarrassed about why you did it. If you can only be a little bit patient with your spouse' characters of engaging in an affair they get disgusted with each other quickly, and because there is nothing that binds them together, your spouse returns to you.

Be understanding and look past that lack of character; be better than your spouse who cheats on you by ignoring what he or she is doing, looking beyond those circumstances, and planning ahead. If you can, advise your spouse to protect him—or herself, and pray unceasingly for God to save him or her from dying in sin. Then pray until your spouse is cured. Only God will heal that not separation, not divorce or nagging. God does not accept divorce, even when one member of a couple has been caught red-handed in an immoral sexual act. Some people may bring up the topic of physical health, and I advise you to protect yourself. Thank God there has been great innovation in this. Jesus said to forgive one another, and he did not specifically say which sins should be forgiven or not. Forgiving is not like a menu to choose from regarding what to forgive and what not to; Jesus instructs us to forgive not once or twice, but no less than seventy times seven. Therefore, even unfaithful spouses should be forgiven.

For a husband who finds it hard to forgive his cheating wife, this is a challenge that you need to overcome. If you are innocent and haven't ever cheated, thank you. There is power within you to overcome the evil spirit your wife is listening to, and deserting her is choosing defeat. Remember, *"Husbands, love your wives, just as Christ loved the church and gave himself up for her"*[40]. If only you could stop being selfish and see how the church has frustrated Jesus, and yet He died for the church. However, you as a man haven't died for your wife; how then have you demonstrated your so-called love? I use the metaphor of dying for your spouse to mean knowing what faults he or she has but going on with the relationship as if nothing happened while helping him or her get rid of the behaviour. Cover up for your cheating spouse, and when that person regains his or her senses, he or she will recognize your kindness. If nothing else, do this for your kids; don't hurt your children by showing them that their mother was unfaithful. It is still a loss that you chose her for a wife without thoroughly investigating her character. Now that you are in the middle of the situation, raise your eyes and your voice to Jesus and ask him to change her. Divorce is self-defeat, even in a case where you yourself caught your spouse cheating.

When your spouse decides to leave you for someone else and the two of them live together, it is best that you do not interfere. Leave and find the strength to settle on your own. During this time, replace him or her with Jesus and tell Him how you feel. Jesus understands the pain of rejection, and He knows how to deal with it. Make sure that when your spouse pays you a visit and hopes to have sex with you, do not give in, but welcome him or her as a good friend. Make him or her feel cared for with a right heart, and deny sex; this humbles the person, and he or she will respect you for that. Such people will try several times to win you over, but do not give in. In your marriage vows, you said you would both leave all others and remain separate, committed to each other, but now that one of you has gone against this vow, you have to wait until God directs the steps of the one who went astray. Most people are fooled when their strayed spouse returns for a visit, but when you give in, know that you are encouraging him or her to feel desired in that way, and after a short while, he or she leaves again. Once your spouse is like this, all you need to do is pray for his or her soul. He or she could die anytime,

Notes:

[40]   Ephesians 5:25 NIV

because being involved in the emotional lives of two people is dangerous; some end up going into witchcraft, which is also harmful. The devil only desires to steal, kill, and destroy.

This person's mind is split; he or she is never satisfied sexually and, therefore, very sick. Just learn to understand, accept, and be patient with this; expect change to happen anytime. If you have prayed, know that Jesus Christ is working a miracle for both of you. When such a person is delivered at last by the power of the Holy Spirit, only forgiveness can bring happiness back to your life. If it is happening to you, my friend, it is normal. Do not give up on your spouse. Many couples have reconciled after many years of going separate ways; whoever took your spouse is just using him or her, and your spouse will be dumped when that person is done, leaving your spouse helpless. When you pick up your spouse from that filthy place, your demonstrations of love must and will be true. When someone has good manners, finances, and health and everything is just perfect, everyone would want to associate with that person. In this situation, it is very hard to differentiate liars from true friends, but when challenges come, the liars cannot stand the test of patience and acceptance. If you sincerely love your spouse, decide to pass this test; even if that person does not realize what you're doing, you will have done your part, and God will reward you. Otherwise, you and your spouse lied to each other, and you are no different from all the other mockers. Try to be more understanding than ever before; your cheating spouse may be together with someone else, but both are insecure about your existence; they are not free or comfortable and will continue to feel ashamed. Doing away with that shame would be returning what does not belong to them. Unfortunately, some people fail to manage the spirit of rejection, and when the stray spouse wants to come back, you are nowhere to be found because you have also become involved with another person.

The reason for forgiving him or her is simple. It's not only because you need to be careful before making any other decision but also because you are a person who understands your purpose in life, and you know that through unfaithfulness, your treasure could be eroded away. Your stubborn spouse took you before the Lord God, amidst relatives and friends, and said "till death do us part." Remember, then, that your marriage is a treasure that you may have to guard with all the strength you have. As the Bible says, *"Guard what has been entrusted to you. Avoid the pointless discussions and contradictions of what is falsely called knowledge"*[41]. Fascinating Womanhood by Helen Andeline, says: "Now let's remember, we are talking about love here. A man can easily be attracted at a sexual level to a promiscuous woman . . . But he could never love her. It is important that we understand this difference. Sexuality in a woman can stimulate lust, but it does not arouse love in a man. Love is awakened by wholesome, feminine qualities, such as sympathy, purity, cheerfulness, trust, and dependence." With faith in prayer and by carrying out your roles well, God will help you through infidelity. He knows it is your right to be supported in this situation.

If you do not take the initiative to forgive your spouse because of the embarrassment he or she made you go through, the devil builds a barrier between you two, and it becomes difficult to reunite. That is why the faithful one must be vulnerable to show forgiveness and be good to the strayed one, to draw him or her back into the damaged relationship. You need to pray hard for God's guidance; the world will fool you with excuses to let go of what seems bad, but if you give in, it will steal your treasure. A person in this state needs someone with true love, and if your love is real, it will help you activate the power to forgive.

iii. Learn to Give Your Spouse's Needs Priority

If we would choose to serve others before we are served, life would be more meaningful. Imagine a family where the husband gives priority to his wife and kids, the wife gives priority to her husband and kids, and the kids give priority to their parents' needs. In such an environment, peace would reign. The family structure was created by God, and nothing can change that design if we wish harmony to prevail. The husband and wife are the king and queen of the family, respectively. Just as the king would get bitter when denied what is rightfully his, so would the queen. It is important to pay attention to other things, but priority should be given

---

Notes:
[41] 1st Timothy 6:20 ISV

to others in your family, not yourself. If your decisions are self-centred, you are a burden to people in your life. A king (husband) or queen (wife) needs wisdom; there are challenges that go along with the role, and it is a treasure that should be enjoyed here on earth. It is therefore important to understand that status goes with responsibilities, and if you want to be given due respect, please carry out those responsibilities and do it well.

Of course, God should be number one for all of us, but here we are talking about your roles in a family. A woman is given the status of a wife, homemaker, and mother because of the man she marries, and a man is given the status of a husband because of that woman, not because of where you were born or anything else. Count it as a special blessing. When you were still waiting, you yearned to get a spouse, and now that you have him or her, you take everything for granted. This is a mistake; get out of your comfort zone and demonstrate the loving words you spoke when you were asking her to love you. Identify each other's potentials and help develop them. That is when your relationship becomes productive and your life becomes more meaningful. Share your dreams and develop an action plan to achieve them. Do not live like competitors; you can share the joy when you each succeed.

Learn to honour each other. There is no success where dignity is absent. I am sure that God blesses you more when you honour each other. How could one say he or she loves and honours God, whom he or she has never seen but fail to honour his or her spouse? If you give love unconditionally, it destroys all the plans that the evil one had for your marriage. Women should know that if there is a great blessing that God gave males, which even male animals fight for, it is honour. Being honoured gives them confidence, and that confidence gives them courage to perform their role in a better way. The secret every woman should know is that in their daily tasks, trying to make ends meet, men are hit by a number of challenges and setbacks; these make men feel defeated; they regain their momentum to try again from their wives. This is done repeatedly and it becomes their life. Every man needs a woman's support; when you comfort him, he feels you are worth keeping by his side. Men might not say much about the challenges they face, but when you can accommodate your husband's weaknesses and failures peacefully and maturely, you attain the privilege to be treated as his queen. It discourages a man when things don't work out as he had planned, and all he needs is a word of encouragement and someone to tell about of his problems. He is seeking comfort, and a lot may be left untold. When he comes home, leave everything else and attend to him; identify what he needs and offer it with a loving heart.

Unfortunately, some women complain "What about me?" It's like they are bartering: if I did something good for him, he must do something for me in return. That would be nice, especially if you had informed your husband that you expected a return for what you did. However, he might not realize your intentions. Have a loving nature; true love is not paid for. Even when he does wrong, you must still think positively and continue to act properly. Some of these values may appear traditional, but when we lose these traditional virtues, marriage loses its true meaning.

iv. *Identify Each Other's Roles*

Just as every business has a contract that defines what each party is expected to do, the Bible defines the attributes of each role in a family. Genesis 3: 16, Ephesians 5: 22-25, and 1 Peter 3: 1 all demonstrate that a woman's God-given roles are mother, companion and homemaker, whereas man's God-given roles are defined clearly as leader, provider, and protector. Every woman is urged to live a life of unceasing prayer such that the man that is meant to lead, provide for, and protect her family is guided by the spirit of the almighty God. If he is not guided by God, he will be guided by the devil; there is no in-between. If you understand this secret, pray for your husband and trust that the Lord will direct your husband's steps. In fact, it is your primary role to help him; I hope you are not going to ask "How about me?" It is commonly said that the family that prays together stays together, which sounds perfect, but if it is not possible, each of you should play your roles and leave the rest to God. If your husband prays for you, that is all well and good, but if you haven't prayed, do so and allow him to lead; accept where he takes you, and stop worrying. This is sometimes very challenging, because as a grown-up with some coins on your own account, you had a plan of what to do and where to go. You may find that accepting everything your husband says to you is illogical, but it is important that you do so. Being a wife involves being obedient to your husband and making sacrifices if they are necessary. If you have a better idea, don't push it; first, implement his plan, even if it fails. Don't rush to state your ideas, especially if he has not sought them out. You need to practice patience and understanding to reserve your own wisdom and implement what he has suggested, and then bring the alternative when he needs it. When you bring that alternative, bring it slowly and gently, not with a know-it-all attitude. Try it out; it works. Consider these words in light of such a situation: *"I tell you the truth, unless you change and become like little children, you will never enter the kingdom of heaven"*[42]. Jesus meant a lot by this, but as women in this circumstance, we need to pray and have confidence in our husbands if for no other reason than because God gave them responsibility, and He is never wrong. After allowing him to play his role in making decisions and planning, surrender all the provisions you have. If you are the bigger breadwinner, this is all the better for your family. In my opinion, managing finances is not a God-given role for ladies. By this, I mean the decisions regarding where money is spent, not who physically pays the bills. Many marriages have problems because the husband is not given the opportunity to make decisions regarding where the money should go. A man may fear asking his wife to give him her salary, and the lady thinks she can use it the way she likes; after all, it's her sweat. This is true, but it's a foolish perspective. Very few men will open up to ask you to combine your earnings. A man may feel embarrassed to ask his wife for her earnings, but when you are wise and use a shared account, leave the decisions up to him, and then he will know that you are telling the truth when you say you care for him and can be trusted.

Some ladies refuse to surrender their salaries because it might be given to a mistress. Whether this happens or not, if a man has a mistress and wants to give her anything, he can get it no matter what; he can even steal or kill. There is one story of a man who killed his two kids to marry his mistress; one person said some men see life only by what their sexual organ desires. Treating unfaithfulness by withholding finances displays a lack of confidence. After all, money will not give you peace of mind,

Notes:
[42]   Mathew 18:3 NIV

which is what you need; it will worsen the matter. I still insist that play your role properly and leave the rest for God to decide.

Whether you earn more or less than your husband, you are still his companion. If you were created to be a companion, then you need to accompany your man towards his vision. If he is visionless, support him by praying first and advising him wisely. He will get revelation from God for how to manage his home. By the fact that God made him male, he will have masculine insights and strengths, but they may be buried in him because of circumstances. These obstacles can be dissolved by your prayers. If he has a vision and you have the provisions for it, pass the provisions on to him. God gave him the insight for where to take you and your children.

To the brother who is never confident or satisfied and is selfish, extravagant, and a thief to his own family members: what makes you feel that way? The money you waste should have made you the biggest millionaire in town, and the time you waste should have made you the best thinker of your city. However, the people you associate with do not even appreciate your efforts; they know you spend money on them because you have it and it is very understandable to them that you are doing it out of foolishness not actually love. You have ignored your loved ones, those whom God put in your life to take care of because you claim your parents didn't teach you any better. You have frustrated the nice-looking girl you lied for a long time until she fell for you, thinking she found a man that would push her to another level. What is your role in her life? You are a mess, but she has been so patient with you. Can't you see that? Why don't you decide now that you will be a responsible husband to her?

Your wife gave birth to kids who do not even know the role of a father because they have never seen you do anything for them. When you go to pick up your own kids from school, teachers keep you at the gate while they call the children's mother to ask her who you are. Oh my God, imagine that! You sometimes forget your kids' names but still consider yourself a father to them; how can you feel you deserve their respect when they grow up? You waste your time hanging out with people who will not even visit you when you are in trouble. Maybe you can't see it now because everything is perfect with your life, but when you are jobless, sick, or in prison you will understand how you wasted what is valuable on the wrong people. Unfortunately, when you reach home, you pay little attention to what your family needs. You yell at your wife, abusing her with all kind of nonsense the devil put in your head. She still perseveres, hoping God will change you, but you still cannot understand. She has taken on the roles of both a woman and man in your home because you cannot play your part of providing, leading, and protecting. You abuse them for even the little that you do give them; they are frustrated by living under your provision, but because that's where nature put them, some persist and others run away. Your own flesh and blood have become street kids; why on earth should you be living? Alas, the good news is that you can become a better version of yourself right now; just change direction and give up the harmful things you are addicted to. God loves you unconditionally. Life can still be good, and love can still prevail in your home.

The problem here is that some of us bring lists of what we want in a spouse and hide the traits or weaknesses we have. This is very unrealistic. When you do this, think of the way God sees you when you kneel down to pray. This selfishness needs to die so that we can achieve God's goodness. This is another circumstance where we are required to develop the childlike faith that Jesus speaks of in Mathew 18:3. If you are a money-minded girl, know that this is a wrong attitude, but you can change and become a good girl. If you have a good career, do not let those benefits shift you out of your God-given role as a wife. Earning more than your husband does not change your role in the home. It is important to understand that no matter how much income you earn, your role is still to be a companion to your husband. You are a blessing to that man, and all you have are his blessings; surrender and let it be this simple. I am confident that you made your choice of a husband within the will of God, although you may not have known that it's His will that you are a married woman. If you start praying for your husband's character today, your husband will become considerate and fulfil your wishes. We have this funny saying: "a husband is someone else's kid." It's true! I doubt whether anyone would be happy getting married to her brother. If you apply it in this context, it means we belong to our husbands more than we belong to our brothers. That's why we leave our blood relatives' house. If we lived with our brothers forever and do not adapt, we would still have the same misunderstandings with them as with our husbands because of our different roles and traits as identified in "Men are from Mars and Women are from Venus"[43]. John Grey suggests that couples can use this model to improve their relationship.

v. Be Submissive

Now that we have known our roles as women, it's important to know the character quality that can help us perform better in these roles. This is none other than being submissive to our husbands. Being submissive means allowing him to take control in your relationship. More specifically, it means allowing him to make the decisions and complying with his wishes. If we don't get down to the roots of this attitude and ask God to help us sincerely behave in this way, it will be very hard to carry out our roles. This is what the Bible commands: *"Wives, submit yourselves to your own husbands as you do to the Lord. For the husband is the head of the wife as Christ is the head of the church, his body, of which he is the Savior. Now as the church submits to Christ, so also wives should submit to their husbands in everything"*[44].

According to the secular opinion on submissiveness, most people say, "It's changed a lot." Some don't think showing the same kind of preference for submission is normal anymore. They think that if there is any room for submission, it should be of a different quality and to a far lesser degree than tradition would hold. Some say the change has been gradual but that it's happening. Others believe there's still a place for submission, but our current generation has made a pretty large separation between itself and the previous generation. Some people feel that this degree of change represents a greater separation than the previous two or three generations had from their predecessors. These people believe that there are a number of things that men simply can't get away with saying anymore. They don't

---

Notes:

[43] John Gray, *Men Are from Mars, Women Are from Venus* (New York: Harper Paperbacks, 2004)

[44] Ephesians 5:22-24 NIV

give examples of this, saying that it would be counterproductive to do so, but they say there are certain attitudes that were once normative but are now discouraged and viewed unfavourably by men and women alike. They believe that there are still some men who would like a wife who is generally submissive, but they think we've reached the point where we have to search for those men instead of finding them everywhere.

Likewise, men have reached a point where they have to search out a woman who will go along with them instead of finding her wherever they look. Some people think this was a little different twenty or thirty years ago, when this situation was more normative among women, but men took a little longer to come around. So for a while, it was increasingly normative for women to be dissatisfied with a generally submissive situation, while most men continued to prefer it or at least be okay with it. Society generally thinks that has changed now—that it is normative for both women and men to want to work towards each other's best interest and for both women and men to recognize that a male-dominated society is not in anyone's best interest.

We are not talking about every man or every woman here. We are not talking about students, colleagues, or a team made up of both men and women who carry out particular tasks. In these settings, there are policies and procedures, codes of conduct, employment laws, and rules to follow designed by the shareholders, management, or administration. We are talking about husbands and wives who should live in the interest of Him who started this union, God.

It is important to note that some people perform with excellence in schools and in their professions but end up divorced. Others feel like they can perform better in their tasks if they are not married, so they end up single. This is because the union of a man and woman in marriage has special principles and guidelines to follow. These are found in the Bible, and we must follow these in love with the help of the Holy Spirit if we wish to leave behind generations that will continue the desires of God on earth. This union was started By God, and the guidelines to happiness and successful living will come from Him. The character required of a woman here is to be humble and be led, provided for, and protected by her husband. This is submissiveness. Being submissive is not ignorant;

instead, it is very necessary if any woman is to play her God-given role well. When you develop the character quality of obedience, your obedient character will shape your children into obedient kids. This character will help you accept your husband and his direction with ease. Taking care of you is his God-given role; it brings him to the proper position of a man in a home. It is important that if your husband passes away, you do not just sit and watch life go by; you have been to the same schools and developed equally or even better. But when he is still living, it is important you allow him to play his role. If you kept a low profile, it does not rule out who you are or what you know. Instead, it would create a situation where you are his consultant in whatever he does, which is why God put you there.

vi.   Learn to Exercise Your Goodness

Every person since Adam and Eve is born with inherent sin. That's why we need to be born again. Some authors say we are born with a clean mind and a clean heart, but this is not true according to the Bible. What one encounters on earth often just increases the desires of the sinful nature and determines the character of a person, depending on what she or he feeds the mind with. Even if a person is well-behaved but not born again, that person is a sinner. If Jesus came back today, he would deny that person entrance to eternity because he or she is not recognized in the Book of Life. Bad manners are typically brought about by two things: not being born again and the environment where someone lives. Exercising bad manners often start when a person is surrounded by negativity; everything that goes into his or her mind is just negative—to try to defend him—or herself and to seek self-satisfaction in a wrong way. A mind fed on negatives gets totally contaminated. However, it is important to mention that this person does not know that he or she is wrong, because this is his or her nature. Unless he or she finds someone with a different mentality, it's impossible to change him or her. When you talk to this person, all that comes to mind is how to defend him—or herself in words, actions, or attitudes. This character quality needs to be transformed. Examples of a bad environment would be one where the person experiences war, poverty, disappointment, frustration, abandonment, and torture, to mention but a few. It is hard to please a heart that is displeased or disappointed with life. Unfavourable circumstances destroy people and turn them into beasts; however, there is medicine for that: understanding, acceptance, and patience. The only way to help such people is to prevent yourself from nagging them. Instead of reminding them what they do is bad, be good to them, talk to them nicely, act rightly, and pray for them. When you follow these principles, you can help yourself and many others that come your way.

It is important to ignore what is unproductive in life and focus on what you can do to be productive. Looking back may bring you disaster. For example, Lot's wife turned into a pillar of salt just because she looked back. What is gone is gone; perhaps you did not enjoy it until it was gone, but now that you can still breathe, plan ahead and take courage. Do not be stuck in the past; after all, it left you with nothing good. Drop the baggage and think of what you can learn from it, so it won't bother you anymore, and you can move to the next level. You are a new, better creation; make your life more productive and help others.

"Inner happiness is a quality of spirit which must be earned by a victory over our weaknesses and the upward reach for the perfection of our character. It is like swimming upstream. It is found in the great efforts and achievements of life and in faithful devotion to duty"[45].

When one talks of inner happiness, it's because there is also the opposite: inner sadness (i.e., unhappiness). Perhaps you experience this sadness when your heart cannot feel any sweetness at all and life seems meaningless. Life tastes sour. Nothing is pleasing, and you feel even your own babies can't make you smile. You are not interested in anything and you feel awful.

Happiness, in its fullest meaning, is the utmost pleasure we are capable of enjoying in a given situation. To generalize, the term "happiness" in English conveys ideas including welfare, comfort, security, and overall enjoyment of life. Happiness is also awareness that one's status is very

Notes:

[45]   Helen Andelin, *Fascinating Womanhood* (New York: Random House, 2007)

satisfactory, that he or she is in a favourable condition or advantageous circumstances.

Despite a lot has being said about happiness, I found that inner happiness is "the pleasure, good feeling, or comfort felt after achieving something, especially when what you have achieved is of great importance"[46].

For example, consider the following stories from the Bible.

Hannah, the wife if Elkanah [47] felt inner happiness when she bore a son and gave him to Eli, the priest, as she had pledged to God during her struggle with barrenness; it was inner happiness that made her give her son to God.

Ruth got remarried to Boaz[48] after all the challenges they went through with her mother-in-law, Naomi. The women in the city said, "Blessed be the Lord who has not left you without a close kinsman." I am sure whoever looked at Ruth saw beauty in her face.

When the Shunammite woman received her wealth back[49], her hope was also restored.

Esther saved her people, and her uncle was given an important post[50]. She was an orphan, living in a foreign land, but she became a queen. Esther saved her people when the enforcement of Haman's evil plan was going to kill them, and her uncle was soon given an even bigger post. I should say this illustrates that being triumphant gives birth to inner happiness.

Notes:

[46]   www.egraceBiblechurch/happiness

[47]   1st Samuel 1-28NASB

[48]   Ruth 4:1-22NASB

[49]   2nd Kings 4:8-17 NASB

[50]   Esther, chapters 2-10 NASB

For all of these women, there was a point of time in their stories when they underwent some challenges. But they later experienced total renewal of their feelings and thereafter experienced inner happiness. A person feels inner happiness when comparing two different situations in life, where one is extremely bad and another is immeasurably good. When a woman experiences real inner happiness, she can feel it, and the people around her can sense it.

To explain more about inner happiness I will use Mary, sister of Martha and Lazarus[51], as an example. From this, we can see that inner happiness therefore helps us:

1. Forgive ourselves of guilt caused by our past mistakes.
2. Feel love. It makes us love ourselves and take care of ourselves, hence making it possible for others to be attracted to us.
3. Ignore the wrong that others do to us or say about us. For example, when Martha came to complain to Jesus that Mary was making her work alone, Mary was not bothered and did not argue but stayed where she was.
4. Know what people around us want and how to offer to serve them, prioritizing them rightly. For example, Mary chose to be with Jesus, and even when Martha complained, Jesus explained that he was interested in their presence, not food. In the same way, it would be easy for us to identify the needs our husbands and kids in a manner that they will feel cared for.
5. Feel loved and wanted. When Mary came and sat at Jesus's feet, it's because she was feeling loved and wanted by Jesus. In the same way, with inner happiness, we will not fear doing anything romantic with our loved ones because of the total trust we have in ourselves and them.
6. Value to what others do to us or for us because we see things positively.
7. Do great things to others, just like when Mary brought expensive oil and poured it on Jesus and dried it with her hair.

Notes:
51   John 11:1-44 NASB

8. Have a cheerful heart and speak positive words. Because we are happy inside, even what comes out will be pleasing. This creates a peaceful and loving environment for our husbands, our kids, and ourselves.

However, the happiness that we create for ourselves gives us temporary happiness. Only the happiness from our Lord Jesus Christ will be real and permanent. It comes with wisdom and maturity so that even though the environment may appear horrible, your heart will be protected from the external influence, and it will remain happy. This is the inner happiness that the Lord gives.

As a child of God, therefore, you need to cultivate your life to be positive even when things are not going right; that, if anything, is what differentiates us from the animals. One needs to have hope in unfavourable circumstances in order to see a better tomorrow. Proverbs says, *"A cheerful heart is good medicine, but a broken spirit saps a person's strength"*[52]. Instead of clinging to what is happening around you or what happened to you, think of something good you can do. You cannot keep from looking at the circumstances, but you can control what remains in your heart. *"Guard your heart above all else, for it determines the course of your life"*[53]. If you are not selective about what should stay in your heart, a lot of junk will get heaped in there, and when the goodness of the Lord wants to come in, it may not have space. If you have understood that you are a child of God, you can live like one rather than like a slave. Do not allow what is ungodly to dwell in you, but keep filling your heart with goodness, and you will be imitating your Father, as it is written: *"All who have this hope in him purify themselves, just as he is pure"*[54].

Right from childhood, we experience circumstances that frustrate us; these keep building up, and we find ourselves becoming bad. Yet when God created us, we were pure and innocent. These circumstances make

Notes:

[52] Proverbs 17:22NASB

[53] Proverbs 4:23 NLT

[54] 1st John 3:3 NIV

us develop scars in our hearts. It is very difficult for a man or woman holding onto wounds to ask his or her spouse to submit or to love unconditionally. For some reason, the people get stuck in a pool of old hurts and disappointment which do not add value to life. Instead, they steal even the great happiness that the Lord has preserved in them.

Goodness and inner serenity are required in a woman for a man to love her deeply (Helen Andeline). A woman develops inner serenity when she becomes free of scars, pride, and self-righteousness; she always does and says the right thing, is free of guilt, and has a forgiving heart. However, it is hard to develop goodness as a person when you have a lot on your mind that is negative. It is hard to love anybody before you love yourself, and you cannot forgive anybody until you forgive yourself.

Think of anything you think people blame you for and forgive yourself. It is not your fault that you made these mistakes; understand that everyone has made his or her mistakes. If you forgive yourself and move on, life ahead will be so sweet. After that, forgive anyone else that hurt you. The lady mentioned previously, who was caught committing adultery and brought to Jesus, left with mercy, grace, and joy because she was forgiven. But this joy cannot enter your heart until you have forgiven others, so try so hard to forgive those who hurt you. Forgive them for everything, not only some things. If you have a problem with forgiveness, pray about it and God will help you forgive and forget. He is not pleased with us holding onto negative emotions, and there is nothing enjoyable about retaining them in your heart. *"Your attitude should be the same as that of Christ Jesus"*[55]. There's an old saying, "attitude determines altitude" In other words, a positive, faith-filled attitude will cause you to rise higher in life, but a negative, self-critical attitude will only drag you down. It is important to know that our attitude affects the outcome of what we do and behave, and we cannot treat people well when we're being dragged down by the hurts. Do not complain because things did not turn out as you dreamt. Be warned. Proverbs says, *"Better to live on a corner of the roof than share a house with a quarrelsome wife"* and *"It's better*

Notes:
[55]   Philippians 2:5-11 NIV

to live alone in the desert than with a quarrelsome, complaining wife"⁵⁶.
That kind of attitude only closes the door to God's miracle-working
power. The Bible says that faith is what pleases God. Understand that
He's trying to work in your life, but you've got to stay on His side and
have faith. Otherwise you will pray again and again, but when God is
not answering your prayers, it may be that you are delaying Him because
you have not obeyed and cultivated a heart that can receive the goodness
of the Lord. *"Therefore I tell you that the kingdom of God will be taken
away from you and given to a people who will produce its fruit"*⁵⁷. God is
pleased with character and attitude, not experience and skills. Work on
your attitude and receive His goodness; all He wants is for your heart to
practice his goodness, and He will handle the rest.

vii. Enjoy Being a Mother and Wife

Mother—Being a mother is a blessing that no one can give you but God.
The kids that you are bringing up need to feel proud of you, regardless of
whatever circumstances you have gone through. It is so important, and
you are not alone. God did not leave you with those kids so they would
suffer in your hands; He is with you, to help you bring them up in a
manner that is pleasing to Him. They should not be a burden to you,
and they should not be left alone to suffer in someone else's hand while
you are still living. "Train up a child in the way he should go; even when
he is old he will not depart from it"⁵⁸. It is very disappointing when they
are grown and you want to be associated with them, yet they did not
grow up calling you a good mother. When they call you by both names,
you get bitter, yet you were hiding from your responsibilities even though
you were in the house. What will you tell the Almighty if you reject your
blessings like this? My sister, we will have to give an account for what
we received when the time comes. Even if it may seem hard, pay the
sacrifice; there are rewards here on earth and in eternity. It is enjoyable
after the struggle, when you are victorious. As mothers, we illustrate the

Notes:
⁵⁶ Proverbs 25:24 NIV
⁵⁷ Matthew 21:43 NIV
⁵⁸ Proverbs 22:6 ESV

power of sacrifice, just like Jesus sacrificed. We can say, *"I have revealed you to the ones you gave me from this world. They were always yours. You gave them to me, and they have kept your word"*[59]. The will of God is for us to be true disciples of the most high and true followers of Christ to do his will, bearing more fruit. *"This is how my Father is glorified, when you produce a lot of fruit and so prove to be my disciples"*[60]. It is not by one's profession, but by pursuing a holy life that the character is tested.

If because of challenges you are planning to desert your own kids for fearing to sacrifice for them just remember that none of these kids asked to be born, and you probably were not insane when you gave birth to them, for heaven's sake. What gives you the pride to walking down the streets of any city in the world when you have not told your son or daughter goodnight before he or she goes to bed and good morning when the sun brightens? What are you living for? What is beautiful in your life? Please, sister: you still have that chance if you are still breathing. What you are going through is normal. Many have seen the worst but sacrificed their happiness for their calling. *"The temptations in your life are no different from what others experience. And God is faithful. He will not allow the temptation to be more than you can stand. When you are tempted, he will show you a way out so that you can endure"*[61]. Ask for forgiveness, and go back to your home. Live with your kids and their father, your husband; they need both of you. *"Do not be overcome by evil, but overcome evil with good"*[62]. If you have taken the children away from their father, soon they will start asking you why. Don't be surprised when they tell you that you were the bad parent. Motherhood is the most noble and important work on earth. It is very frustrating when women do not recognize this because of the way they are brought up. Endure the difficulty but enjoy the wonderful satisfaction of raising happy and secure children.

Notes:

[59] John 17:6 NLT

[60] John 15:8 ISV

[61] 1 Corinthians 10:13 NLT

[62] Romans 12:21 NIV

Wife—This role is given to a woman by God himself, and we should enjoy it. *"The wise woman builds her house, but with her own hands the foolish one tears hers down"*[63]. There is also an old saying that, "he who has a better home has a better wife". This implies that even our ancestors without a Bible knew the role of a woman. They did not say she should be highly educated, from a rich background or a dynasty, or tall, short, or dark, but she should make a good home. A good home involves a number of many things, but Proverbs 19: 14 tells us where she can be found *"Houses and wealth are inherited from parents, but a prudent wife is from the Lord"*[64]. A good woman is God-fearing and imitates the desires of God in nature. She hears the word of God and puts it in action, regardless of circumstances. This woman submits to, respects, and agrees with her husband; her children are God-fearing, and her home is organized. We cannot achieve these things when we stay at a distance from God, who gives wisdom in everything. We need to get involved with the word of God and act on it and live in it; as we do this, we shall be called a good woman who is from God.

Sometimes you meet a very smartly dressed lady on the street, but when you ask her if you can go to her place, she looks down and says nothing or lies because she is worried about how her home looks likes. Others are not even bothered when visitors find their homes in a mess, but when they give you a glass to use, you prefer drinking from a bottle because you trusting a brewing company more than the cleanliness of the glass. She is bringing up kids and taking care of a husband in that home. I don't think being smart is bad, but let it be applied to everything in your life. Make yourself, your husband, your kids, and the environment of your home smart. This is not why women are failing in marriage, per se, but it is not feminine to live in a dirty, messy home. If we organize our homes well, the devil cannot attack us from that angle.

It is important to make friendships. Among these, make female friends, but be very selective in this; not everyone will suit you in character. Visit each

---

Notes:
[63]   Proverbs 14:1 NIV
[64]   Proverbs 19:14 NIV

other and do things together. Confide in each other. Develop your talents. Accept correction and learn from your mistakes. Out of these relationships, we learn from each other and make good homes that are pleasing to God.

viii. Practice Wisdom with Your Feminine Power

Thank God for the changing times; nowadays, girls and women are no longer confined to doing housework and mothering. They are free to study to the level they can afford and take a job of their choice. Having equal rights with our brothers has exposed us to numerous benefits, especially when they are well-utilized. We must consider the way we claim our rights and display feminine traits when we are in unfavourable circumstances. It is important that you do not misuse them, focusing on what you may have achieved, and losing your divine purpose rather than using achievements to reach your destiny. A lady who understands the power of femininity within her would use these strengths to save her marriage and to serve others in need. God gave women the potential to serve others, but some of us deliberately do not want to serve others or do not know that we possess the capacity to do so. Women's strengths are not physical but intellectual. This intellect helps you to use your feminine power and strength softly; after analysing and understanding what is desired, and you come up with what is required. Ladies who shout about their physical rights have missed the point; the softness of our bodies demonstrates how we should also use strategies gently to get what we want. Prevent yourself from nagging and haggling with those around you; it will not yield much. Instead, act gently and kindly and do what is required, no matter what it takes, and you will achieve what you desire. In *Fascinating Womanhood* Helen Andeline calls these women angelic characters, means one needs to think like an angel in order to act like one through serving others.

Femininity, also called femaleness or womanliness, is the set of roles, behaviours, activities, and attributes associated with women and girls by a particular culture. Femininity involves being different from a man. It means embracing the fact that you are a woman and expressing it in a way that is consistent with your personality and tastes with the goal of being noble. The word feminine is related to the word female, so it relates to the words and grammatical forms referring to females. That's the strict definition, but it means so much more than that. Like all things, it depends on what a person believes. For a married woman, there virtues that you should endeavour to possess simply because you are a woman with a divine vision. These qualities are expected of you regardless of age, profession, background, and so forth.

Many women in the Bible misused their female characteristics. Eve, the wife of Adam, was fooled by what she heard and saw ignoring the instructions from God, her creator, and her actions led to all the following generations of humans being born into sin. What do you do when your husband is away? Who keeps you company when he is not with you? Examine yourself and find out whether it is the devil. He might not come in the form of a snake this time. The devil changes strategies, but his objective remains the same. John 10: 10 says his goal to steal, to kill, and to destroy. We should learn from history because otherwise, it repeats itself.

Job's wife was not supportive when her husband lost all his possessions and was very ill. She got fed up of the circumstances and disgustedly uttered discouraging words to her husband. Job was a true servant of God and did not obey her when she said to him, *"Do you still hold fast your integrity? Curse God and die"*[65]. He replied, *"You are talking like a foolish woman. Shall we accept good from God, and not trouble"*[66]? In all this, Job did not sin. So many of us have failed to say what is needed at the right time; I wish we would learn to keep quiet instead of sounding foolish; I also wish every man was as loving and faithful to the Lord as Job.

When Sarah, Abraham's wife, saw that she had become old and thought that God could not use her to bless the world, she advised Abraham to have a child with her maid, Hagar, and later she became jealous. Her actions have caused conflict between the descendants of the sons of Abraham for centuries. This should show us how most of the problems we have on earth originated from the actions of just one woman; therefore, I think we have to be careful with what we say and do.

Next, let me talk about Rachel at length.

Notes:

[65] Job 2:9 ESV

[66] Job 2:10 ESV

Rachel was the beloved wife of Jacob in the Bible[67]. Her sister, Leah was also married to Jacob, but Jacob loved Rachel more. Rachel was the younger and more beautiful sister. Their father was Laban, brother of Rebekah (Isaac's wife). He practiced divination and kept idols in his home; he acknowledged the existence of the true God but did not honour Him as God through his actions. Laban deceived Jacob and tried to cheat him; he didn't give his daughters any part of their dowries. Rachel came from this background when she married Jacob, and she had some of his father's traits. She exercised them on her father, sister, and husband, but she became a believer later, after having made many mistakes.

- Rachel was barren, and she demanded that Jacob give her children, forgetting that only God can give children. She became a nagging woman, asking Jacob for what he could not give her. This made him become insensitive and rude. They both desired to have kids together, but the words that Rachel spoke did not activate Jacob's masculine sympathy; instead, after all the anguish and insensitive words, Rachel resorted to using mandrake plants, most likely as a fertility drug.
- She stole idols from her father's house and brought them with her when the family left Laban's camp. She had lived with Jacob but was not satisfied with what he believed in. The desire to keep her father's idols made her deceive Laban to conceal her theft.
- She made a foolish plan to obtain children through her maid, Bilhah[68]. This was similar to how Jacob's grandmother, Sarah, had given Hagar to Abraham to bear a child[69]. *"Rachel's servant Bilhah conceived again and bore Jacob a second son. Then Rachel said, 'I have had a great struggle with my sister, and I have won'"[70]* I should say this was actually foolish of such a thing because she had not gained anything at all but instead had increased her worries.

Notes:

[67]   Genesis 29:18, 20 NASB

[68]   Genesis 30:1-8 NASB

[69]   Genesis 16:3 NASB

[70]   Genesis 30:7-8NASB

Bad Character Qualities

- Rachel was not content with Jacob's protection or provision, and that's why she stole her father's idols.
- She was not satisfied with the love Jacob had for her, and she nagged him to give her kids.
- She was a liar because of her dissatisfaction.
- She was jealous, and this led her to making her husband commit sin (Jacob obtained kids from maids).
- She wasn't friendly to her sister because of her jealousy.

Consequences

None of Rachel's children carried a spiritual promise from God, despite the great love that Jacob had for her. Rachel was robbed of life at an early age. Leah remained with Jacob after the death of her sister, and Leah's sons inherited spiritual blessings. Descendants of Judah became kings, and others were priests (Levites). Following Leah's achievements can create inner happiness in any woman, despite the challenges. It required her to offer moments of sacrifice, which some of us refuse to offer.

Some of us have traits similar to Rachel's. She had a husband who loved her very much. That was a tool that she could have used to make a home, and the rest of the blessings would have found her, but her pride wouldn't let her do this. Examine yourself to see what you have led your husband or kids into because of your selfish nature, stubbornness, and foolishness. The Lord Jesus can restore your character; go to him humbly, with the desire to change. He knows your heart and can save you.

There are four identified secrets every woman should know:

> "*Secret 1: Your husband cannot meet all of your emotional needs.*
> *Secret 2: Your husband has emotional needs that are just as important as your own needs.*
> *Secret 3: Your husband was designed by God to be the leader of your family.*

Secret 4: Most men truly want to make their marriages work"[71]

It is important that women know how to help their husbands handle discouragement. When men are discouraged, the source of this challenge may be failure to get a job for a long time, losing their loved ones, being harassed by their boss, workplace politics, or losing something they put great effort into. Men also feel discouraged by not being appreciated, when they are sick, when they feel they are not offered enough respect, when they are rejected, when they are not admired—the list is so long. It takes a God-fearing man to wait upon the Lord to change the bitter situation; even some God-fearing men lose their patience in such circumstances.

Because of the marriage vows and because of her role as a suitable companion, a woman needs to be near her husband when he feels discouraged; she understands the situation and does the right thing accordingly. This is how you put into action the words in the vows you made before God and people. Unfortunately we like the wedding gown and being covered in veils, but when the time comes to put these commitments into practice, life becomes bitter. If you are not sure what marriage is all about, learn this first. After you know the roles of a wife, then you can put on the gown and the veil; otherwise, you are just being stubborn in your ignorance.

Now that it's time to put the vows into action, you need to be careful not to make mistakes. Remember, when life is better, richer, and healthier, anyone can stay there until death do us part. When he calls you sweetheart, honey, and queen, carrying you around the house; everyone can compose a song and sing it a thousand times a day. When circumstances turn around, you will understand who was sincere and who was not. God always allows these things to happen so that our true character—the true power and wisdom of femininity—will show up and be activated.

---

[71] Shannon and Greg Ethridge, *Every Woman's Marriage* (Colorado Springs: Waterbrook Press, 2010).

These characteristics showed up in Abigail when Nabal[72] was drunk and refused to give food to David's men out of arrogance.

They showed up in Hannah, the wife of Elkanah[73], when her rival, Peninnah, kept mocking her barrenness.

They showed up in Queen Esther, who replaced Vashti[74] and had to save her people.

They showed up in Ruth, the daughter-in-law of Naomi[75], who cared for the widow after she lost her husband and sons.

All of these women practiced wisdom, humility, and being submissive to God and to their husbands; that's why they won their battles. Because they were humble before the Lord, He gave them wisdom on how to handle their bitter situations. Even now, they are remembered for their feminine power that changed bitter situations. Everyone has the potential to change if he or she chooses to do so. Unfortunately, some of us have little or no patience and understanding in our hearts, so we get fed up when situations are bitter, and we start looking for escape routes. The story of Job again demonstrates how we sometimes fail to offer support to our discouraged husbands despite our vows to do so.

Although Job's troubles were great[76], we can observe that:

> Job's words were not evil.
> Job was sincere.
> Job tried to respect God.
> Job still gave honour to God.
> Job was a genuine servant of God.

Notes:
72   1st Samuel 25NASB
73   1 Samuel 1:1-27NASB
74   Esther 1:1-22; Esther 2:1-23;NASB
75   Ruth 1:1-18NASB
76   Job 1 & 2 NASB

Job lost all his wealth; his children died and he became ill, but
Job still praised God.
Job still trusted God.

Naturally, we should sympathise with people who are sick and about to
die. We should care for them. And we should show them that life is a
gift from God. But Job's wife did not have a sympathetic character. At
this point, Job needed a wife who would use her feminine power and
wisdom to admire the courage he had to maintain respect for God. He
needed a wife to sympathise with him. His heart needed to hear soothing
words with hopes of a better tomorrow. Unfortunately, all that his wife
saw was death; she had lost kids and wealth, and her husband was so ill,
and maybe she thought about getting another man who was richer and
healthier. She was hopeless and saw no future or life in Job. How many
times have you behaved like Job's next to your man?

Job's wife was truly overwhelmed by all the misfortune they experienced,
yet Job needed an understanding lady who would accept him regardless
of how he appeared. She failed to realise this and did not understand why
her husband continued to honour, praise, and thank God after all that
had happened to their family. His wife saw him with carnal eyes; he had
been so rich and famous but was now poor and ill, left with nothing at
all. That's why she wished for him to commit suicide. Some families are
demolished by misunderstandings between the husband and wife amidst
challenges because of lack of maturity. Some men go to prison because of a
certain problem and when they are released, they find their wives married
to another man or pregnant from a fling. Because things are not working
out at that time, the devil fools you with a solution: to do away with your
spouse. What is the level of your wisdom? Whether hard circumstances
are because of one person's mistake or an accident, just allow time to pass
and look at the other side of the situation. Divorce is self-defeat. Learn to
be patient and instead learn from your bitter situations.

In such situations one needs someone with common sense to provide
assurance that change is a fact of life so that he could gain some courage
for the days ahead. His inner person was still so good and godly; he could
look on the good side despite the challenges they dealt with. As noted
previously, he still honoured and praised God. Unfortunately, when his

wife looked at his sick and stinking body, she took him for granted and had no respect for human life. If you have the same attitude as Job's wife, please change; our God has the power to restore.

Just like everyone else, Job had a very good past; his wife would have recalled this and attributed it to his proper guidance, and he still had this because it came through honouring God, and Job still honoured him. She should have recognised that his guidance, protection, and leadership had earned them a lot; she could've been confident that things would change for better and they would be well off, as before. Instead, she devalued all that Job had been and done, the good life she had enjoyed with him, and all of a sudden felt Job should die. She would at least have learnt to pray, and she could have gone in her room and privately prayed to God and come back to comfort Job; but because she lacked a prayerful life, she talked instead. If anyone reading this has a similar character to hers, Jesus can give you wisdom for what to say or do; ask for forgiveness and start afresh. Tell your husband you were not aware you were hurting his feelings. Perhaps you saw the truth of the circumstances, but you need to have the eyes of an angel. The Lord, who gave you the riches you once enjoyed, is still the same God, and He never changes. You are just in a test, and it's only for a while; just like Job experienced, everything can still be restored, and you will be better off.

His wife should have said to him, "I love the way you put your confidence in the Lord." This would have given Job a little more strength, regardless of the terrible illness he had.

At this point, his wife did not bother leaving him, and I am sure Job lived in the days when God said that man shall leave his family and live with his wife, and the two shall be one; I wonder whether Job's wife remembered her matrimonial vows. Job's wife wanted him to forget these things. It's like she was fed up with taking care of a crippled, sick man and did not need him anymore. Do you really understand your role in your marriage, or you are just holding a title and you cannot really live up to the requirements? Revisit your character; it requires transformation.

It was important for Job's wife to understand that though Job was ill, he was still a man of the house, so he needed to be recognised and respected as a leader. He had a doctrine that he wanted everyone to follow despite his illness, obeying God. But his wife did not see this, and she got fed up with Job's trust in God, and she discouraged him further by asking Job to curse God and die. I ask you to look at your spouse's problems or challenges as his sickness, which needs to be handled with maturity and understanding. That's when you will understand the message in this book. Otherwise you will never understand it, but you cannot run away from the consequences of your actions.

I don't see anywhere in the Bible where Job asked his wife for her opinion. It seems to me like she did not know when to talk, what to talk about, or when to keep quiet. Such a person would hardly understand what to do and when to do it to help his or her spouse. In some circumstances when a man is the one suffering, a wife needs to just be quiet about the whole thing and reserve her comments. Many men have made mistakes because of wrong advice from their wives. The devil wanted Job's family to show God that Job would no longer have trust in him, and that's what his wife urged him to do. The devil made everything that Job had perish, but Job did not deny God his supremacy and treated his beloved wife gently despite her bad advice. Maybe additional curses could have come upon woman, but Job was wise. We should seek God's guidance or keep quiet, because some men are wiser than us, even in the midst of problems. We should be careful as wives when our husbands are discouraged; if we are not careful, we might tell them to do what the devil wants, yet God places trust and confidence in them.

People should understand that when wrong character is exposed, it's not for the sake of condemnation but rather to help them understand what they can do to activate good character that they would not have known otherwise. We all learn through mistakes; and perfection only comes after many trials or is only found in heaven.

Many people in couples, including the author of this book, have chosen to apply the principles it contains and have experienced tremendous change in their marriage. Unfortunately, some happily married couples keep quiet about these things and do not want to share what they've learned with others, but if they did, many would give it a try. Imitation of something good breeds more goodness.

PART F.

Value Transformation

There are many ways different authors may define these two words, but I would say that if you want something, you should look like it, so that when someone looks at you, he or she may easily identify you. Unfortunately, some people have insincere personalities, and this is not healthy for a wife, mother, and homemaker.

i. *Your Appearance*

As much as you take care of others, it is important that you also have time for yourself. Mind your body and be healthy. When your husband married you, he was physically attracted to something he saw in you. Try your level best not to lose it, including your style of dressing, your weight, and whatever else makes you stand out as a person. There are tasks God has ordained you to do by virtue of being a woman. It is important, therefore, that you maintain good health to pursue them. If you do not do certain things, no one will do them for you. Maintain your ideal weight by practicing regular exercise and sound nutrition. Think about what you will feed your family on, and try to have a change of diet with well-prepared food. If you have difficulties in this area, ask friends or read relevant books. Some of them will be knowledgeable about the things you don't know, and they can help you. Smile from a cheerful heart always; it polishes your appearance and attracts him to you, yet it does not cost you anything.

ii. *Activities*

I talked about roles before but not exhaustively. It is important to understand that there are roles men and women can both do but there are others strictly meant for men and others for women when they are living together. They may help one another because of the changing ways of life and expressions of love and care but when actually if all factors remained constant some would be described as feminine others as masculine. In families where one of the two travels a lot or for instance serves in the army, the one remaining in a home does it all by himself, but where both of you are around, there should be proper segregation of duties otherwise a couple may collide or misunderstand one another.

Several women are complaining that their husbands are like visitors in their own homes. That they least contribute to the home affairs and even do not appreciate what the wives do. Sorry about this, but if your case is similar to these ones, look into your schedule and see whether you have not violated the trend of action into masculine roles and he opted to let you carry on as he watches. Some men have the potential to do even more than we expect but wives are not letting go of masculine roles. If you are from a home especially of single parents or where your father never provided enough at home you may think that all men are like your father yet your husband is different. Some know that providing for their homes is a masculine task and want to do it but their wives do not want to live in their husbands 'means. When a woman does not want to live in the means of her husband and refuses to give him the more resources she earned the man withdraws to let go. This is where most husbands get resources saved for mistresses and what is legally yours is taken by someone else.

In general, a couple should identify what each person should do and not try to take the other's tasks. Sometimes when wives do men's roles, they feel there are two masculine creatures in the house, and scientists put it clearly—"like poles repel, but unlike poles attract each other". We should leave doing masculine activities to our husbands even though we should be helpful in general. Sometimes you meet a woman driving a nice car, and she tells you her husband bought it, when actually she found the money to buy it. However, she lies about this because it feels good when the man brings a car into a home. Her desire for him to buy it for her makes her lie. The logic is simple: if you have the money, pass it on to him, and if he finds something necessary, he will definitely buy it. These activities may include heavy lifting, repairing the house, paying rent, and any other activity that makes him feel like a man. Your life should be different from that of a feminist or a spinster; don't hesitate to feel the presence of a man around you. This is why God put him in your life. When you do what he is supposed to do, then he loses his pride as a man. He might cherish what you did and even respect you, but he cannot feel attracted to love you or cherish your personality. A woman develops love for a man by having gentle reliance on him. This is sometimes prevented by the provisions you reserve for yourself. The money deceives you, and you imagine you can make it for yourself. True, you are satisfying that desire, but you are killing your emotions. That's why some women continue lying to their friends, saying their husbands bought them things that they actually bought themselves. Learn to be dependent on your husband and surrender all the provisions to him; he will shower you with a lot more. If a woman has faith like a child, this is a noble virtue for her to have as her husband's companion. Display openness, innocence, humility, trust, dependence, and a carefree charm.

There are differences in men and women that make us feel attracted to each other. However, some women make the big mistake of doing men's roles, thinking this would attract love and respect from their husbands, but this cannot work. If it worked, it would just be physical attraction, but he may feel disgusted by the things you are doing overall because he sees that you are taking his position and you want him to worship you. He wants you to appreciate him for his work, but when a wife does masculine tasks, he feels useless next to her. He will come in, see what you did, and just keep quiet; you might wonder whether he has eyes to see or not. Sometimes you even ask him, "Did you see what I did?" He will simply say yes and keep quiet. If he is more open, he will ask you where you got the money and the story ends there, or he might say you are too wasteful. It's not that he is too blind to see that what you did was fabulous, but it threatens his masculinity. If he encourages you, the next thing on your agenda might be to change your residence without him knowing, simply because you want to give him a bigger surprise. Woman, instead of all that, just clean your bedroom, change the blanket arrangement on your bed, add a few candles to the bathroom, and serve a well-prepared dinner. When he comes home, he will carry you in his arms like a baby and tell you how he married a prudent woman. Compare the amount of effort in the two activities. The message here is simple: play your part wisely and nicely.

iii. Mind Your Language

Elder Marvin J. Ashton once said, "The tongue can be a sharp sword. This sharp sword hurts feelings, demeans others, destroys relationships, and harms self-esteem". It is surprising that some women shout when they are actually just conversing. They say everything rudely. We must examine ourselves to see if we do this; if you don't know, ask your husband or your kids (if you have them). If you haven't traumatized them, they will be frank and tell you. Some men out there feel like hiding when their wives start talking, but they don't have a real reason to because until you die, you are named after him. These men choose to love us and they should, however, women can say things in a wrong manner that is not so appealing to the man. If you ever do that, it may never leave his mind. This is why it is very important to think before we speak. This is very important if you are interested in having a peaceful and happy relationship with your husband. *"It is better to remain silent and be thought a fool than to open one's mouth and remove all doubt"* said Abraham Lincoln. When you stop to think before you say something to your husband, ask yourself whether it is kind, true, or necessary, and try to imagine how it would make him feel. Then either say it or forget it. *"The heart of the righteous weighs its answers but the mouth of the wicked gushes evil"*[77]

The Bible[78] tells us about the power of the tongue and how dangerous it can be when wrongly used. *"When we put bits into the mouths of horses to make them obey us, we can turn the whole animal. Or take ships as an example. Although they are so large and are driven by strong winds, they are steered by a very small rudder wherever the pilot wants to go. Likewise, the tongue is a small part of the body, but it makes great boasts. Consider what a great forest is set on fire by a small spark. The tongue also is a fire, a world of evil among the parts of the body. It corrupts the whole body, sets the whole course of one's life on fire, and is itself set on fire by hell."* This is why, when we speak, we should try our best to phrase it in a positive and loving

---

Notes:

[77] Proverbs 15:28 NIV

[78] Proverbs 18:21 & James 3:1-12ESV

manner. Sometimes what you want to say is not what the other person wants to hear, but getting irritated or angry will not make it any better. Having a positive attitude and a loving, sensitive approach will make a difference. If you are not in a position to speak positively and lovingly to your husband, it's better to remain silent and plan another day to say it or leave it out of the conversation.

Every human being, man or woman, needs a moment of silence on his or her own sometimes. It is important to know when your husband is at that point so that you do not interrupt him with issues to solve or discuss. When men are concentrating on difficult tasks they don't like distractions. It is important to know when he can pay attention to you and when he is busy or preoccupied. Unless it's a lifesaving matter, it's important to allow him to be alone so that he may attend to his personal issues. When you have been given a chance to speak, know when to stop talking. Talking to your husband too much will not change a lot, and he will not be convinced by the number of comments you make or the number of examples you provide him with. Instead of making him restless or anxious, say the main points and reserve the rest for prayer. God will lead him to ask you what you were saying, and your wishes will be taken as final decisions. Remember, the Holy Spirit speaks for us, so do not waste time on speaking. When you explain a lot, it is like fighting on your own, denying the Holy Spirit's role. Again remember, *". . . for the battle is not ours but God's"*[79]. Some men don't want to embarrass their wives by asking them to keep quiet; we also need to be sensitive and watch whether they are still interested in talking or if they would prefer to be silent. That is how a couple will enjoy each other's company.

It is important that we do not forget our role of companionship, because that is how we prevent violating our calling as wives, homemakers, and mothers. Think of how it would feel if someone you brought home was calling loudly, giving you orders, shouting at kids, giving remarks, whistling in the house, and nagging you with issues—to some people it is really disgusting. This is why manners are important in a home. Women

Notes:
[79]   2nd Chronicles 20:15ESV

should have good manners, choosing to phrase our words positively and lovingly, convey cheerfulness, be clear, have confidence, be gentle, and laugh freely and often but not loudly. The way we walk and the way we look at things can either be good or bad for our husband. Be graceful, accommodative, compliant, flexible, and relaxed.

iv. Clothing

A woman should make the most of her femininity when she chooses her hair style and what to wear. These things mean a lot to your husband. Choose colours that are appealing, depending on where you are going and what you are going to do. Imagine him getting there before you, and put on what you want to wear; think of how those you will find will think of your husband when they see you walking up. A man can be impressed by the way you appear in public. In whatever you do, be conscious of his relationship with you. Your clothes mean a lot to him and to the public. Unfortunately, he may not tell you what he thinks because men normally do not criticize women's appearance. Some women dress like men and think that's the most appealing. Very few men (especially African men) would not love to see their wives' bodies visible to the public. Masculine nature is too possessive; no one man would want to share his wife with another. So, even knowing that other men saw their wife's body parts is annoying to some men. In the same way that exposing the parts of your body that should be covered may not be appealing, dressing in something that covers you like a shapeless blanket may also be unappealing. If possible, discuss this with your husband and respect his choice and yourself.

v. Making Requests

The Bible[80] says we belong to our husbands, and our husbands belong to us. However, if this privilege is not used well, it may not be productive. Learn how to requests things from him in a loving and considerate manner. Let him see some level of concern in you, not like a consumer

Notes:

[80]   1st Corinthians 7:4 ESV

or a commander in chief. Take the example of Queen Esther[81]. When she wanted to make her request to the king, she did not jump up to him and tell him of the problems that her people were facing; she first prayed about it and organized a nice dinner to which she invited the king. After attending to the king very well, she made her request, and there was no way the king could reject it. By praying, Esther had received God's favour and wisdom on how to approach the king in a way that he begged her to tell him anything she wanted. This is what every woman should do: go to God first and then attend to her husband's needs, and then seek an opportunity to say what you want. It is unfortunate that some men are given a list of issues before they even sit down from a long day of work. Even to some of you who have joint account, well done, it's the best way to manage finances but you should not disrespect him because you surrendered your earnings. Even if his level of prioritizing may be different than yours would be, do not shout at him. Respect his choice and suggest your ideas peacefully.

We have seen that even what we have earned or otherwise gained should be surrendered to our beloved husband. Yet, there are certain things that we need, and sometimes we run out of provisions. This is the best time to groom your husband in his role as a provider. However, do not just come in and shout, "The charcoal and beans are gone, and even my mother needs food." There is a way of saying things and choosing when to say them. Get organized first, welcome him with a smile, get him something to eat and drink, and allow him some time to rest. May be there is something he wants to say to you. When he is relaxed, bring your list of needs with gratefulness and confidence in him. It is his role, but you need to get all you want. Some of us are fed on potatoes and beans because we ask poorly, and part of the money that we would enjoy is taken to the supermarket to be spent on someone else. Be careful, or you will die in a rented house with your kids when new construction is getting completed for your neighbour. If you are not careful, if God takes your husband before you, his sisters will introduce you to his other kids, who are fat and healthy when yours are dying of kwashiorkor.

Notes:

[81]   Esther 4: 16 & 5:1-5 NASB

Be polite, be gentle, and ask for what you want. This will not take away anything from you or reduce you to something else, but it will give you what you want. Some women think they can do everything by themselves. True, you are able to, but what brought you to his home in the first place? Mothers who are too vain or proud have caused their kids to sleep hungry or become malnourished, even though the children's father could provide for them. Feminine pride has made women live in misery; dear sister, look at the problems you have in your home and see whether it is caused by pride that has not been surrendered to Jesus Christ. You are behaving the wrong way and irritating your husband, and you will not get what you want. After being turned down, we repeat the saying "a man is another person's child." Yet, if you had just behaved right, you would get as much or even more than your father gave you.

A Letter from Nyatsi
(Nyatsi is a Setswana word for "Mistress"[82].)

Firstly, I don't want this to seem like I don't respect the boundaries of marriage, but as a nyatsi, this is my point of view. Ladies, we don't intentionally go hunting for your husbands. We meet them like you meet people every day: through friends, at the supermarket, at work functions, hell, even on the side of the road. We don't always know from the get-go if the man is married, because a lot of these brothers don't wear rings or come with a stamp saying "taken". Half the time he's alone, and there's no trace of you, even in his car! It takes a well-trained eye to spot traces of another woman, such as perfume on the seatbelt, weave strands, hair oil on the headrest, and so forth. My job in your relationship is to give him a break from reality. Yes, you and the kids are real, but so are the bills and school fees and work stress, and I'm where he de-stresses. I know my place—trust me, I do. I know to keep quiet when you call while we are together, and I know not to spend on his credit card but to ask for cash; all this is to protect you, yes you, from pain, humiliation, and suffering, I get

Notes:

[82] Adopted from an email exchange with a friend from Botswana>

a tired, frustrated man and send you a well-rested, happy man. Thank me; don't disrespect me for it! Calling me won't change the fact that my clothes are expensive and my car is paid off. It won't change the fact that my university fees are paid and I get to go to the weekend conferences or boys' nights out. Swearing at me won't change the fact that he grips my headboard when he rocks my world and screams like a girl, something you probably don't even know about the man you married. You don't know the effort we put behind our little rendezvous just to keep your pudgy ass happy and feeling secure. Trust me, the more you come after me, the more he wants me, the more money he spends on me, and the more intense our sessions get.

A true nyatsi will never ask him to leave you; instead she encourages him to stay with you even if you have messed up badly. We never consider getting pregnant out of the fear of having to deal with your sour face for the rest of our lives. So, relax, your kids are priority numero uno, even to us. We pick out the toys and clothes he shows up with and we encourage bonding time. Consider yourself lucky if you find my number—at least you know he's taken care of when you're tired, and he's gonna come right back once we are done refurbishing my apartment. Oh, and trust me, I do the fighting for us. It's my job to make sure it's just us two; any others will be dealt with severely by me, so don't ruin your manicure. I get a weekly one, so it's okay; let me do it. I respect you; hence, I stay away from family functions and make sure I take all my stuff out of the car when I was there. I don't call after he's left the office because I know it's your turn. I have my own things; the rest is just a bonus for having a kind and sharing attitude. I'm a professional with a great job and I earn enough. I don't have time to tend to a full-time relationship; hence, I don't mind when he goes home to you.

My advice to you, "mama'se khaya": stay in your home, and don't pack your stuff and go tell your mom how you failed at being a wife; it just makes you look stupid and weak, and our man needs strong women around him. Look after your kids, tend to your home, and cook those hearty meals you are so famous for; I can't cook with these nails. Don't ask about me. He's just going to lie and toss and turn in bed, thinking about me in the Victoria's Secret set he bought me for Valentine's Day. Let me be, and I will leave on my own accord one day. If you don't, we might just trade places, and you will be saying "izinto zabantu" or say that I consult sangomas. I don't; I would rather spend that money on expensive holidays with our man. Truth is, I make him feel good, I'm a reminder of when he was young, and I do all the things you are afraid to do or won't do because you believe you are past that. I'm forever young and I compliment him; you suit him. Trust me, honey, there is a huge difference. I respect marriage and all it stands for. That's why I'm doing my part to help yours stay together, so don't think I don't. I respect the nice thing you have done, and I love your kids too much to hurt them. Don't cry over me or what we do. Let it be, play your part, and I will do what I'm supposed to do.

Yours (and your man's),
Nyatsi

On a serious note, if it is true, should such a short-lived relationship destroy the future of a family? If we failed to avoid it, can't we learn to overcome? Our use of language has failed many of us. How do you communicate?

Learn to approach your husband and say, "Please, can I . . . ? Please, will you? What matters is not the touch but the tone—the please and the smile. You are being gentle, humble, and trusting him to do it. These acts will loosen the account that you did not know about, and you will see money coming to you even when you do not ask for it. Wherever he is, when he thinks of you, he recalls the tone of your voice saying "please" and thinks you said it that same morning. Your children will look their best, go to the best schools, and your mother will be treated like his own, instead of you having to steal and hide things to send to her. However, you need the Holy Spirit, my dear sister, to help you achieve this character. Unfortunately, some ladies treat other men this way but have failed to do so with their husbands. Even your husband has the potential to provide for you with love; just shift your actions to the right man.

If you doubt this, remember how you used to ask your father to do things for you. Sometimes he would say no, but because you acted rightly, you would get what you want. Just do the same with your husband. They are both from the planet Mars; you will get what you want. Even if he does not have it immediately, he will work hard to get what you requested. Even if it's a proposal, it will be accepted or granted. This is not simply about asking; it shows that you respect his authority and you enjoy his roles as a leader and a provider, and he will enjoy pleasing you. Taking a submissive posture in asking means you area recognizing him as a leader and a suitable provider, which grows the feelings of love he has for you. When you awaken those feelings in him, he goes the extra mile to satisfy you.

If you ask and do not receive what you want, appreciate that he was there to listen to you, thank him genuinely, and then close that topic. Let him see your positive attitude and allow life to flow normally. He is human; he will think about what you said, and later in the day, he may surprise you with it and additional gifts if he can. But do not ask, suggest, bring alternatives, demand, argue, and start nagging. This is irritating. In this case, he will just give you something little to get rid of you, and every time he is away, he will recall your nagging tone. He will get in the habit of thinking, when she nags, I will give her this. You can live a forceful life in your own home. But asking submissively will get you even more than you expected.

There is no need to explain why you need what you want when you ask submissively. When God gave men the role of providing, He placed this noble character in their hearts. "A man loves a woman more when he can do things to please her and when he can sacrifice for her"[83]. That is why we should have no worries about surrendering what we earn to them. When we give them our earnings, we plan together and develop our economic status; and when we need something, we are shown more love. On the other hand, refusing to give up our provisions makes us live

Notes:
[83] Helen Andelin, *Fascinating Womanhood* (New York: Random House, 2007).

a self-satisfying life and it robs us of the peace of mind and our husbands of the joy of pleasing us.

You should ask your husband for anything and everything; accept love, tenderness, being taken by him out, or gifts. These things hold more meaning when they come freely from him without you asking. This is when a woman feels her value. When he gives you a gift, please show genuine appreciation. Please don't behave like you expected it, and do not start asking about its price; thank him, and appreciate it. Even if he bought something you don't like, keep it, and after time has passed, you could ask him for money to buy what you do like. Unfortunately, some women do not buy certain things because men know their favourite brands and sizes, and when husbands bring what they find shopping, women start asking about the prices, comparing them with what they saw at a neighbour's house. Please appreciate; your husband brings those gifts to you out of love.

It is so unfortunate that some of us essentially rob our husbands. Because we don't trust them, we do not share with them all we have but we want what they have. The truth of the matter is that some men waste a lot, but the solution is not to hide from your husband. If you do that, you are not living an honest life. If he wastes resources, make some time and organize a talk about it; if after that he does not change, leave him alone about it. Concentrate on your role and leave him with his; next time he gets stuck, it will teach him a lesson. Stop nagging him; he is a grown-up, and he has plans of how to provide for his home. If you do not agree to his approach, pray and ask God to change him. Prayer gets you through life in so many ways. Pray for the Holy Spirit to guide your husband on how to provide for you, lead you, and protect you, and you will remain peaceful.

vi. Treat Anger with Wisdom

It is normal for every human being to get annoyed, because life is not a bed of roses; but what you do when you are annoyed is what counts! Anger should not overcome your wisdom. Decide at once whether what has angered you should steal your peace and the peace of those around you. Though he is the one you are annoyed with, this does not remove him from his position as a leader, provider, and a protector of your home. Have some respect and wisdom. Maybe it is a misunderstanding. Find strength, remain positive, and find time to talk about it with honesty and truth. Giving reasons and comments about your annoyance may not do you any good. *"A worthy wife is a crown for her husband, but a disgraceful woman is like cancer in his bones"*[84]. As long as you remain pleasant, he may not be offended. It is important to always remember each person's role in every circumstance. This will guide you and protect you from going astray in your words, thoughts, and actions. There is an enemy of peace, peeping into your home to steal your peace. Don't take anything for granted; a very small incident in your life together could be an opportunity to destroy your marriage. *"Be well-balanced [temperate, sober of mind], be vigilant and cautious at all times; for that enemy of yours, the devil, roams around like a lion roaring [in fierce hunger], seeking someone to seize upon and devour"*[85]. The devil is around, perhaps in the corner of your well-furnished sitting room or bedroom, and as you move, he moves with you and deploys different agents for different issues of which you might not be aware. Don't be afraid, but be conscious of every step because anything can be his tool.

Using logic and demanding explanations will not solve your problems. Understand that you can do nothing alone, but you can do all things with the power of the Holy Spirit. This is another time when having the humble faith of a child can help. *"And he said: "Truly I tell you, unless you change and become like little children, you will never enter the kingdom of heaven"*[86]. A child is helpless without his parents; just run like a child to the Father and tell Him with confidence what has annoyed you. He knows what is in both of your hearts. The trust you put in Jesus Christ when you surrender your understanding will move him to intervene on your behalf.

Notes:

[84]   Proverbs 12:4NLT

[85]   1st Peter 5:8 AB

[86]   Matthew 18:3 NIV

Nothing can change a man's heart except character. You may not get to this character permanently without the help of the Holy Spirit. Stop using your own logic and look to God, who gave you the home. Children with values are humble and honest, especially in the way they express their emotions. In the same way, you can seek God's intervention. He knows what to do and when to do it. Stop wasting your time shouting at a grown-up; what is impossible for you is very possible for God. If what you are going through is persistent, ask God why. God is real, my sister and friend. He will speak to you, guide you, advise you, and protect you. Even when you are waiting upon the Lord to act, remain positive, cheerful, and acting right; you never know when things will become good again.

There is no issue as your legal rights here. So many marriages have broken up when both of you are innocent. It is better to exercise your right as a child of God than as a wife or husband. Laws and rights come into situations to rescue people from destruction when their hearts have refused to obey God. Why, then, should you wait for the law to be applied, when you can get a password or master key as a child of God? When the law comes into play, as in divorce, you will get robbed of what is rightfully yours. The wife or husband you are divorcing is your own, and maybe you are leaving to go live with another woman or man who will never be honorary yours. Once you are a second wife or husband to someone, it will always tickle your brains that you belong/belonged somewhere else, it is possible to find temporary happiness but no peace of mind. This becomes worse when there are kids involved! Why then should one opt to that? If people separate to get peace is there peace in that really?

One wonders whether such people understand the importance of vows, they once said "till death do us part" and now you are parting before death comes, who should ever take you to be serious in whatever you say. You may give people justifications of why you gave up on him or her but the one listening will tell you, "had you to be a little bit patience, understanding or accepted to sacrifice, he/she would have changed!" Or the listener may just look at you and keep quiet, You cannot justify that to anyone; people and circumstances do change, it's just a matter of understanding and patience.

Despite the challenges we go through, God hates divorce and He is the Almighty, He is the only one who can address all the issues that steal our peace. Jesus Christ, His son, saw the injustice and pain of divorce that were brought about by the rebellion of man and said that neither husband nor wife should separate from the other. Jesus also said that remarriage after divorce is adultery. This is why no authentic servant of God can marry you for the second time when the first wife or husband is still living.

The best advice we have over who wronged us is to forgive, Jesus asks us to forgive seventy times seven 70x⁷ in a day[87], and he did not specify the wrongs that should be forgiven which means we should be like Jesus and forgive all. After all, who are you not to forgive, unless you claim to be an angel living on earth. Failure to forgive may be a sign of pride otherwise; a heart with humility is full of forgiveness and dependent on God. Allow your heart to forgive, pray to God for strength and support to act right, and pray for this weakness. Although there are people who have divorced each other because of unfaithfulness, there are also those who have maintained their relationships regardless of an unfaithful partner. It is important to have understanding in a relationship, because you may face this problem unless remain single. I am convinced that Jesus said we should forgive one another and did not intend adultery to be an exception.

i. He knew you could not get married to angels once you divorced your first spouse.
ii. He knew he had taught us the power of prayer. The Bible says, "Submit yourselves, then, to God. Resist the devil and he will flee from you"[88].
iii. He was confident that he had not left us alone to struggle with the devil on our own.

Notes:
[87] Matthew 18:22NASB
[88] James 4:7NIV

Be careful to ignore the voice whispering to you to divorce because of unfaithfulness; the devil might have observed that you fear unfaithfulness, and it is what he will always threaten you with so that you don't stay in marriage with anybody. Attack him with prayer and bear in mind that the word of God is true. The devil will threaten you, but he does not have the capacity to make you do anything. It is up to you to say yes to him and fall for his threats or say yes to Jesus, and the devil will flee from your marriage. You have both the username and password to everything by prayer, my sister.

Otherwise, remember the principle as a God-fearing woman: you have to accept your husband as he is. This means accepting his weaknesses most of all, because everyone would enjoy his good traits; but because you have to be happy as well, drop those weaknesses at Jesus's feet. Certain things are better left ignored. Try to do this immediately, and then tell your husband in a friendly way that what he said or did is not pleasing to you. When he does it again, don't repeat what you said the other time; just know it's a character you should put on the list for God to handle. Avoid picking on him or counting how many times you have told him you do not like something. You are a companion who should be at peace with the one she is there to serve. The scars of his past might be what make him behave in that manner. After you have identified this behaviour in him, the solution is not to remind him of what he is doing, even though it is not pleasing to you or to God. A man is at his best when he is told of his best virtues; but for the bad traits, it's best to pray and ask God to take away those scars. In a way, sometimes you are just a victim of his past experience. Although it is true that you should praise your husband's good virtues and thank God for giving you a man with such virtues, make a list of all his bad characteristics secretly and take it to God in prayer. You never know when he will change, and you should not cease to pray until the last bad character trait is gone. You will have to pray for your husband from the day you think you should get married to each other up to the day you walk from him to your creator. It works.

Another way of releasing anger is to get busy with some productive work. If you do not have anything to do other than watching what he is doing, go to play sports or take a walk and get relaxed. When we just sit there watching what they do, we shall definitely notice and be bothered by what they did. But when we are busy, we notice our own imperfection, and we understand the pain others go through to get things done. If we understand that our spouse is a person who tries but makes mistakes, we will forgive him or her quickly when something they do does not go the way we wanted it to.

Let me refer you once again to Mathew 18: 3, where we are asked to behave like a little child; it works for people in challenging situations. That is why Jesus gave it to us as a tool to enter heaven. He understands that the principles of going through such a journey require faith and obedience. Even in marriage, we are in a journey to our divine calling, and we need Him to help us to reach our destiny; we need to have faith in Him and obey Him. Jesus Christ does the rest on our behalf. In the same way, therefore, when things are very bitter, the best treatment is to keep quiet, not giving justification in reaction to anger. Even if tears come, let them flow. Even if your husband sees the tears, don't mind, but make sure to say a word that shows that you are helpless and vulnerable, in the softest manner possible. King Solomon said, *'A soft answer turns away wrath*[89]. I'm sure you have read it or heard it before. It really does work. If you feel you cannot do it this way, remain silent. Remember, you are in a battle that needs divine weapons to change a man's heart. This puts him in a position to offer a masculine service to comfort you, making him feel wonderfully. The anger just disappears, and tenderness and love take its place.

Even when he is nagging, kindness and sympathy can make him change to stop that. However, if you are kind and sympathetic and he continues nagging, it probably means some of the principles we talked about are missing in you. Correct yourself regularly. Don't take anything for granted, and don't feel that you are right every time. Sometimes we forget what is right, and the devil talks us into doing things that are not right.

Notes:

[89] Proverbs 15:1 ESV

We need to know when to speak and when not to. Normally, when you want to understand someone, it's best to let that person speak, and then you will better know how to help him or her. After this person talks to you, you know what to add to your prayer requests. It is best to let our husbands say all their angry feelings before we say anything, to avoid the Ping-Pong of words. Even if he says hurtful things, understand that anger can make him say or do things without editing his speech. It takes a wise person to understand that the more you know what is on his mind, the better way you may be able to control the situation and diffuse the anger. Even if he is wrong, listen to him and allow all of his angry feelings to come out. If you are innocent, explain the truth positively without embarrassing or challenging him. This situation may make one cry, especially if you are innocent, but let the tears come if you feel like doing so. This is a vulnerable circumstance. Let him understand two things: you understand how he made the mistake, and you don't hold it against him. But when you are guilty, remember he has the right to get angry. You just have to be humble and softly tell him that he is right, and you are sorry for doing something silly, and then ask him for forgiveness. His anger will disappear, and his love for you will increase because of your humble nature. This is another feminine way to save a marriage in a wonderful manner.

vii. Giving Advice

It is best to go with your husband to a church where each of your virtues can be replenished. When you are in church, the preacher will preach, and each one of you may pick out what concerns him or her about each other, and you find that you do not have to repeat for him what he already knows. If he does not go to church, make sure you visit proper families which he may feel like imitating. If he does not want to walk with you, invite them to your home when he is around. Otherwise, be careful when giving advice to your husband. Give it when you are asked to do so—when he asks your opinion or when you are giving motivational advice. It should be occasional; otherwise, it will feel like you are minimizing his perspective. When you see that he is about to make a big mistake, try to advise him, and if he takes your advice, that is all well and good. Even then, when you give advice, you need to be polite and not use challenging words like: "I know", "I think", and so on. If he does or does not follow your advice, just keep quiet and live a life of prayer. Your prayers will protect him and guide him. Do not be forceful; it will not work at all. It is best to say nothing and let your husband have free reign as a leader. "It is normally better for us to put up with the consequences of a few bad decisions, than to risk wounding our husband's sensitive pride, and causing resentment"[90].

When life is so challenging, you must be strong. *"If you faint in the day of adversity, your strength is small"*[91]. Sometimes you may be ignored for no reason. Do not get bitter; bitterness will steal your chances of demonstrating kindness. Your husband ignored you because he is annoyed about something that he doesn't have confidence to talk about, and you must find it out in order to help him. You can only make him say it by being nice to him; therefore, apply your feminine techniques; smile, remind him of something good he did before, and he will understand you are not faking it. Then come closer to him and touch him in some way. If he is distracted, he will turn to you. If he is flirting back, repeat it with good intentions. Straighten his tie, touch his shoulder, stroke his hair, or sit on his lap if you are alone. Catch his attention and say something that is not too important so he will pay attention to you. These same acts can be helpful even when he is being too serious and starts lecturing you about things that you feel are not important. Even then, don't stop him; leave him to speak, but act in the same manner. Look him in the eye, smile, and say something funny. This might not make sense as you read it, but it makes a man calm down instead of giving excuses or explanations.

However, if he is very bitter and wild, keep quiet and pray for the Holy Spirit to intervene, except to say you are sorry. If you don't fight back with words or actions, he will calm down. Sometimes, the situation is threatening, but as you keep quiet and pray from your heart, calling for the protection of the power of the blood of Jesus, the situation will

---

Notes:

[90] Helen Andelin, *Fascinating Womanhood* (New York: Random House, 2007).

[91] Proverbs 24:10 ESV

definitely calm down. After its calm, do not bring it up immediately as a topic to discuss, even if you are innocent. Wait and see if he will realize that what he did to you was wrong, and do not underestimate anything. Know that you need to pray unceasingly until he is saved. If your spouse is violent, remember that he or she probably grew up seeing parents or neighbours behave that way and doesn't know how to handle anger. Learn how to manage it well before it grows beyond the limit. Such people have good intentions, but they were affected by their background, so you both have to decide whether your past is going to defeat you or not. You can talk about this when you're not in the middle of a quarrel. In a wise way, ask each other how you can solve your disagreements without fighting, and after that talk, share a nice meal, to help your spouse forget the bad character attributes you talked about. Getting a nice meal after discussing such a nasty character shows that despite the nasty behaviour, you still respect him or her. If the husband is the one whose attributes are discussed, he will take your advice and agree with whatever you say; he will hate what you hate; among your hates is his fight, and so on. It's a little like training a beast. I am sure that the people who tame wild animals use good techniques, because when you show it the bad, the beast is an expert. Divorce is self-defeat; should you break up your marriage and change your divine calling and marital status because the formerly loving guy has turned out to be a beast? Definitely not. Be wise and understanding; you should realize that he would have loved to be called a good guy, but the circumstances he grew up in did not allow that. If you love him like you claim you do, help him to be good like he should be. However, if you are pretending to love, you will have no patience to do that, and you are defeated battle.

We talked of a number of principles in this book, but it is important to understand that the challenges in a home are from the devil himself, which he deploys as weapons against you. The devil's objective is to steal, kill, and destroy a family[92], like he did to Adam and Eve. God loves families very much; that's why he created man in his image and gave him a special place to live in, Eden. The devil hates the institution of family

Notes:

[92]   John 10:10 NASB

very much; that's why he uses all the possible tools to destroy it. All the bad things you see taking place in your home are not because you or your spouse is bad; it is the devil coming to destroy you. When you see anything that is displeasing, know that your home has been attacked. Wage war against the devil, not your spouse. At this point, your spouse needs you more than other times, your children need your support more than before, and you need wisdom to defeat this mess in your home. Stop blaming people and call upon the almighty God. Fellowship with the Lord more than ever before, and remain peaceful once you have prayed. Forgive your spouse and do only good things. This is possible when you know who you are and what you stand for.

God is aware of the challenges we are going through; He is not like a snake which never takes care of its offspring. He is very loving and caring. The reasons why we often don't enjoy total happiness are that either we are living in sin, or He wants us to grow to another level for the purpose of His power working in us. Think about yourself and establish why you are not enjoying total happiness in your life. Then act accordingly. If it is because of sin, reconcile with God, leave that sin, and enjoy life. But if the devil is attacking, resist him, stand firm, know who you serve, and act right; at the end, you will rejoice with victory.

Sometimes experience suffering because there are people around you who need to learn from what you are going through. God's ways are so many, and only He knows why we are who we are and where we are. When Paul and Silas were put in prison[93], there is no doubt they experienced great pain. These men were beaten like Christ was beaten—without cause—but kept rejoicing in their hearts. Rejoice when you are being tortured innocently, because Jesus understands that very well. You do not even need to explain you were innocent; He knows this when it happens. He went through it, and He knows how it hurts and how disgraceful it is. He wants you to identify with Him in that pain, be patient, act rightly, repay good for evil just like he did, and wait for perseverance to do its part.

Notes:

[93] Act 16:1-40 NASB

Praise and worship were very unusual sounds to hear from within the prison in Macedonia, but Paul and Silas chose to praise God, and they created an unusual environment around that area. I am sure the other prisoners got pissed off at first but later enjoyed the music. The other prisoners had never seen or heard of this, and I am sure they threw around comments, criticizing the "new guys" who had hopes. Maybe you, like Paul and Silas, can make people around you see the difference of a mother and woman who fully embraces Jesus. The power of Jesus Christ manifests in you during tough times, and He never gets stuck or fails to find ways out. If the gates of death could not hold Him, would the gates of the Macedonian prison hold back His Spirit in Paul and Silas? They could not. In the same way, if you have embraced, Jesus nothing can contain you.

Maybe you have been praying for so long, and you are worn out and tempted to give up. It happens. Peter and his friends fished the whole night but caught nothing. They gave up and were washing their nets to go away. It was daylight, and they knew fish is caught at night. They had applied all the experience and knowledge they had of the profession, but they still got nothing. Maybe you tried all possible ways to save your marriage, but now it's no more; the way you see it, you cannot live with your spouse anymore. Try Jesus. Look for Him and invite Him into your heart, whether to a greater degree or for the first time. Shout out, "Jesus, I want to see you". When Zacchaeus wanted to see Jesus, he climbed a tree[94], and Jesus paid attention to him; He went to his house and ate with him, and Zacchaeus's life changed. Even if you don't know Jesus, shout His name and invite Him into your heart. He never fails; when He is in your heart, things around you will obey you.

When Jesus came to Peter's boat, he took them to deeper waters, and because they cooperated they caught too much fish[95]—more than ever before yet they had totally given up. In the same way, involve Jesus in your trials, and obey His word, and you will be blessed. He wants to

---

Notes:

[94] Luke 19 NASB
[95] Luke 5: 1-11 NASB

get you out of the shallow water to show you that you can do much more than you ever thought. Divorce is a consequence for a lack of cooperation with Jesus Christ. Jesus never fails or lies, and all those who trust in Him are never put to shame. Jesus can mend a broken heart if you give Him all the pieces.

PART G.

Conclusion

Dear friend, the Bible[96] determined the role of a man as the leader of the family. God the Almighty said this, and His word is final, so we must try to accept it and instead adjust to fit in the requirements of what is required of God's plan. Just like spoke night and day into existence, so he declared man's position in a family. His word is law, and no other law will change this, not even circumstances or achievements. Just like light spreads in the morning, when a male baby is born, a new leader of a family is born; even if that baby grows into ignorance and does not fulfil his responsibilities as a leader in his family, it does not change that fact. God will still look at Him the way He wants it to be. To help a man is to try to channel him into his role, not replacing him or reminding him that he failed. Remember, he fails because of ignorance, and that is not by choice. If you are any better, you should make decisions that strengthen the relationship, not ones that destroy it.

Choose God's way; his plans are better than ours. He advises, "The truly wise woman has built up her house, but the foolish one tears it down with her own hands." This wisdom is demonstrated by our actions, which originate from the heart. The head contains some major parts of the body. It holds the brain, which connects throughout the body to enable understanding and internal communication. The face is also on a person's head; it provides his or her identity, eyes for direction, ears for understanding the environment, the mouth for communicating with the environment, and the nose to inhale and exhale the air we need to survive. Likewise, the role of a man in a family is to provide, lead, and protect, as described by many. However, there is need for flexibility in order to have an excellent life, because those other parts need to act

Notes:

[96] Ephesians 5:22, 1stCorinthians 11:3, 1st Corinthians 11:8-10. NASB

properly when the brain asks them to do anything; the heart must give a positive response for the routine to go on. Just imagine if your legs did other than what you needed or they didn't move; what if the hands did not put food in your mouth, and so on; everything would be chaotic, and so is a relationship.

Dear male friend, being a provider does not only mean financially, it means more than that. Your contribution is expected towards emotional, spiritual, physical and mental well-being of the family. As a protector in the family also a man has to ensure security of your wife and children from anything or anybody that may abuse her self-esteem and self-worth. As a leader, you have to take the initiative in designing what you want your family to look like not just to sit and wait to listen to whatever comes your way. When you set standards what is not welcome will remain outside

If you do not understand that your wife needs your protection you whine about your family situation and she definitely gets disappointed in you and her altitude towards you changes because she will be trying to get secure on her own. What she feels towards you will influence you. This is reaping out of your action. It is dangerous to live in dirty surrounding clean up, if you are any better and turn her into a helpful person, you will benefit a lot. A person does what is in his or her heart otherwise; whether you like it or not if you do not take care of her she will influence your character. A couple is one person, they may be two different physical beings but they are spiritually one that is why divorce never separates them.

When you are marrying a second wife or husband, he or she comes along with all his or her past. And managing someone's past where ex-husbands and wives are involved required extra effort that sacrificing temporary happiness while you pray for God intervention to transform your own into a better person. I should advise every male that if you want to be a honoured manager maintain your own recruits when they are promoted to the next level and start counting how many bridges crossed they will see your support at some point in their live. Your hassles will be limited and when they recall their past they will honour you for life.

Keeping in mind that you are two different beings bound together physically, spiritually, and emotionally will help a lot when you tangle. This is a complex process that needs a high degree of patience, understanding, and acceptance. This is why, if there is something that you feel should change in your partner, you need to pray and ask God to do it for you, and life will be easy. You need to pray because nobody is a mistake on this universe; we are all created for a purpose, and everyone needs each other to reach the next level. Maybe your spouse needs you in his or her weaknesses, but if you do not know your roles at that point, that's why you are planning to run away from your responsibilities.

I advise you to fight the good fight as God stands with you. For my sisters, I say that we are not like women of the 1900s. A lot has changed in our favour. We get out of the house and go to school, and we can be more productive than simply living a life of mothering. There are many opportunities for us, and we need to do them; however, circumstances should not steal our divine calling as women. We need wisdom to understand what is necessary and required, and that can only be detected by the woman we spoke of earlier. "The truly wise woman has built up her house, but the foolish one tears it down with her own hands "Proverbs 14:1. It takes a wise person to detect the consequences of his or her actions, think beyond the circumstances, and act properly. It takes a wise person to sacrifice when he or she believes in receiving what is hoped for. This is what is expected of a truly wise man or woman in his or her marriage. Anything you find that is unusual in your marriage is a signal for you to take appropriate action to close a loophole; it implies that there is need for an action to close the gap rather than expanding it by running away. Choosing divorce means you are running away from your responsibility to serve and care for the weak and helpless. That person's acts are a declaration that he or she needs help with personality or character traits and wants someone who is better than him or her for support and to help him or her become a better human being, but you are escaping. Yet, at one time you cherished the moments you spent together. Think back and ask yourself, if there is nothing good about him or her, ask yourself why you accepted that person into your life. Think deeply, and ask yourself if you have a heart. If you can act more responsibly than your spouse, you should forgive him or her and stop accusing. Instead, think of a way you can help him or her be a better person; God will reward you for this.

Divorce is self-defence from serving someone in need, and indeed it is self-defeat and dissertation. The primary calling when we decided to get married is a divine calling to serve, and it goes along with the challenges of marriage, which we should fight to win. We should refuse to drop out. Marriage is not a mutual contract; it is, rather, a solemn covenant between a man and woman, with God's seal. It is a tool God uses to teach us the life He called us to live: selfless, serving, respectful, forgiving, caring, and loving; divorce, then, is a failure in these areas.

Marriage is not an association, a company, a cooperative, or a team or group. It means more than that because it is a divine establishment, whereas the others are man-made. When these organizations stop, the consequences are easily manageable. God, the creator of heaven and earth, is the author of marriage guidelines. We should look to Him for our values and to improve the efficiency and effectiveness of our marriage. The secular world takes us in a direction that might not help us achieve our divine calling as married people because it creates escape routes from the challenges of marriage. However, these secular routes do not satisfy our emotional needs or solve the effects of divorce. Children born in these circumstances are greatly affected, and this contributes to the loss of fundamental elements of a strong society. Some legal rights and the options they offer might mislead us if we are continually driven by circumstantial emotions. We need to find out about some of the facts we have disregarded, which some people consider old-fashioned, and see how we can modify them to suit the times. May we know how best to deploy our potentials to be a blessing, not allowing them to steal our divine calling.

My Personal Testimony

My full name is Uwimana Enid Muragira Mutabaruka, an evangelist from Zion Temple Cerebration Center, Kigali, Rwanda. I live in Kigali, Rwanda, and I work at the Central Bank of Rwanda. I grew up in a protestant Christian family, and our parents made us practice a Christian lifestyle. It was like a culture where I grew up, but it was not imparted to me very well because I lived a double life. I knew that I had to pray before I ate, slept, woke up, or went anywhere. I took Holy Communion because I had had sacramental training, and I wanted to be a good girl. I got married after a long-time secret relationship with my husband that had started at a tender age. We are happy with our four children, but this is after great misunderstandings in between that almost threw us apart.

Since my childhood, I was much loved by my parents, but when I got a boyfriend who loved me, you can imagine how lucky I was -so spoiled! In my dreams, I always pictured a wonderful family when we get married. I did not know much about marriage definitely, but looking around at that time, I could not imagine living with someone I didn't feel a marriage kind of love towards. Secondly, I believed my choice of who to marry was personal. I used to see married people who had not made their own choice of spouse, and when they met challenges, I thought it was because they had no love for each other in the first place. I believed that someone should get married because he or she loved the other person and nothing else.

I am sure most couples will find this interesting—the married, engaged, and even those who may be facing challenges in their marriage, looking at it as a sinking boat, I have some encouraging news.

My husband (then boyfriend) and I decided to live together in 1996 because I was escaping from a man twenty years older than me, who my parents had decided should be my husband. I could not submit to that, and later, alone, I married a man of my choice. After some time, misunderstandings in our home began, and I did not realize it, because my Christian background was not strong. I was mixed up with many things: studies, my job, my babies, and looking after my family as well. We were living with family members on both sides, alternating households, and as a young girl, I could not handle all the responsibilities. I started to have problems with my husband; we would disagree on almost everything, and this shocked me. Life went on like this for a long time. I tried to ask him or the family members we were living with what was going on, but no one could give me an answer. When I got tired of the stress and the abusive relationship, I told myself to get out, and I live on my own.

When I found an apartment to move into, I asked my younger sister to look for a pastor to pray for it because she and I were used to the Christian habit of praying for the place you are going, as mentioned previously. She took me to a pastor at Zion Temple Celebration Centre, and the pastor advised me not to move out; instead, he managed to convert me, and I accepted Jesus as my personal Lord and Saviour there and then. He asked me to attend Bible studies on Tuesdays, Thursdays and general services on Sundays. I liked these meetings because they taught what I needed. It was not like an ordinary church of routing readings from prayer books which I was used to but a school of self-transformation. It was like they cleared my eyes, and I saw life in reality. At the services, they explained the word of God, gave us principles to guide us and how to apply them. I enjoyed attending so much that I could not wait to be there. I used to go and stare at the pastor teaching, and I only saw wisdom in the leaders there. I wished my husband could listen to them. I thought and learnt, that Life was challenging because we lacked the kind of wisdom that these men had. I could go home with more hope, looking forward to the future without violence. I understood that if I continued, I would achieve this future. I asked my husband to come to church with me, but he did not agree; he would drop me off and drive away. I started practicing what was said at church. I learnt to invite the Holy Spirit to guide me. I was a learner and of course did common mistakes of little faith that most learners do. Sometimes people around us do not get saved because they don't see the difference between when you were not praying and when you do. I started to identify my own mistakes and rectified them. I made it my daily assignment to concentrate on how I could and should be the best wife ever. I realized how much God loves me, and always begged Him that I should not get to old age when I still have such problems. I looked at my challenges as lessons and believed that when I passed them, He would take me to another level. Many people tell me I was naive, but it worked. I attended church and read encouraging books; I felt that no human being was able to give me what I wanted, but God would. I rejected people with negative intentions, but I did not tell them; I just ignored their ideas.

God will not leave you partially developed when you are focused and you have positive intensions. He instead allows the devil to throw more dust in your eyes so you are able to look further when there is no more dust to throw at you. God wants you to understand the works of the devil in your life so you may chase him by yourself and chase him in others. The devil had come to destroy my marriage for good, and things became worse, to the extent that I started to pray that my husband would disappear from my life. But God showed me that I still needed him and my children. When I felt like I should give up, the small voice whispered to me, "No, Enid, don't give up. You need to do good and think correctly, and I could go on." Thank God I had accepted Jesus as my Lord and Saviour. Thank God I had a church to go to. From that point on, divorce was never among my options. Despite looking, I never found a single verse in my Bible which gave me divorce as an option, and I asked God, "Why don't you save my marriage if you hate divorce?" I did not get an answer, but I stayed positive.

The whispers from the devil always cause fear and said to me that he (your husband) will kill you, to save yourself, just leave the country. But I had read Proverbs 28: 1, and I kept meditating on it: "The wicked man flees though no one pursues, but the righteous are as bold as a lion." I felt confidence and courage to persist. Thank God that Jesus was with me, even though I might not always hear him speak. He had said to me, it was not simple, but if I would be patient. I had dreams that my husband would get saved, despite all the challenges and I convinced myself that that was God speaking to me. After all, I knew about many dreamers from the Bible. I settled down and started doing only what I felt was right. I felt forgiveness and empathy with my husband; I understood the battle was between God and devil, and my husband and I were only tools. I realized there were evil forces around us and settled in for a battle that was both spiritual and physical. I considered whoever talked ill against one of us to be an agent of the devil, no matter who it was. That became my password, and I would listen but ignore their stories. I read my Bible, followed my pastor's teachings, and tested every circumstance by the word of God. Dear friend, you hold the keys to peace if you have Christ in you, for He is the Prince of Peace.

The challenges for my husband and I involved prison, and I looked after him while he was there, respecting him as my own. I was led by the Holy Spirit until he got out. It was not easy for him, our kids, or me, but I was strengthened by scriptures. That was easy for God. When things were at their worst and I was totally fed up and tired, I felt this should be no more, I said to God, "Dear Father, I know that even now, we are still together so end the battle I am tired and fed up". I asked Jesus to guide my steps, and He did. In those days I read about *"the smoke signal"*[97] and related it to my circumstances. It made me prepare for God's intervention. I opted to protect the unity of my family and kept all of us united the best way I could, and this made the devil run away from us very fast. The devil has no weapon against patience and resilience. I am sure he caught the next flight to hell and left all his agents wondering and confused. I learnt many things out of this but most important was;

- God is able no matter what, good all the time and should be trusted.
- God and devil are both spiritual but have ears to listen to your confession, eyes to see your actions, and a mouth to talk; they will tell you what to do but will not force you to do it. It is up to you do decide.
- Whoever you decide to obey, the other finds his way out of your life.
- God and devil have no permanent servants; consistence to serve them depends on the choice of an individual to do so. They both have so many candidates who ever you reject will not remain un served.

Notes:
[97] Kimberly Dawn, 'Shipwreck', *Scent of Faith* website, http://scentoffaith.com/shipwreck.

- Even your own emotions or character can be devil's weapon to fight you or God's weapon to save you. So think over and over it before you take a life time decision.
- Most of all a marriage is worth a sacrifice.

A question may be asked that 'should a person remain in an abusive relationship? I say YES when one has Jesus, situations will change for better.

It is a tense moment where you only need the Holy Spirit and your bible nearby. Do not sympathise with yourself when the Holy Spirit tells you to do something, just obey no matter what, so long as you are sure that it is the Holy one speaking, He never fails. Do not be scared, you are not the only one; many have gone through worse things and survived. What causes fear is devil otherwise nations would not be having security personnel. If fear was something to consider great nations would create robots to stand in for their security. But because battles are there to be fought and won by human beings, there are army men in every country, ready to face anything that may try to threaten their nations.

It is always not an easy task but once it comes, stand firm and face it. It was tense when the three brothers, Sheldrake, Meshach and Abednego, said to Nebuchadnezzar that ". . . But even if He does not save us, we want you to know, Your Majesty that we will not serve your gods or worship the image of gold you have set up." Their character helped Nebuchadnezzar to see the son of God before He was even borne on the earth and his power to save mankind[98]. Please do not give up may be those around you need to know that Jesus is alive and can still save.

It was not easy at all also for the Apostle John who was dipped in boiling oil but continued to defy the Roman magistrate's order with the truth and proclaimed Jesus as Messiah, Savior and Lord. The true love for Jesus was so strong, that he could not give up when he was put in the Island of Patmos to die and rot there. While at Patmos he got closer to God and

Notes:
[98]   Daniel 3NASB

was revealed of the last book in the bible and he delivered a message to mankind[99]. Sometimes God prefers to use us when we are outside the comfort zone. There is no place far from God and it's never too late for him to do you a miracle. May be you also have a message to deliver to mankind and you are sitting on it. May be God saw that the only way to have it delivered will be through your bitter circumstances, please do not fear, and cling to Jesus.

It was tense for Jesus the son of the Most high dying on the cross[100] but today mankind has a Saviour.

Staying in an abusive relationship is a sacrifice born of great understanding and heroism. Soothing divorce because our siblings have done so, is not doing justice to the coming generations who should be advised with words like; perseverance, patience and resilience. It is forgetting the power God the Almighty, who wants to be manifested mightily and in miracles that have to happen here on earth. This is why I would advise those who are in the process to give it a second thought and stop, those who have divorced to revisit their decisions and reconcile. If you truly loved each other it can be mended.

Staying in an abusive relationship is telling fears that 'leave me alone' I know what I believe and whom I should serve. It is a demonstration of character of the Lion in you and the Lion is Jesus. When you have Him, you don't see life in the ordinary but spiritually. There is another dimension that His Holy Spirit will take you and there lies the solutions to your challenges. It will be closer to God, who owns the power and wisdom; there you get the capacity to do things beyond your ordinary strengths. You will understand why you should sympathise with your oppressors, sacrifice, forgive and stay. I wish you would understand that is not divorce that will change bitter situations but the Holy Spirit when

---

Notes:

[99]   Revelations 1NASB

[100]   The passion of the Christ (2004). A film detailing the final hours and crucifixion of Jesus Christ.

you obey. "Strip away all layers of superficiality, religious reasonings and pious pretendings"[101] and you will get what you want from God.

After this experience forgiveness was my best weapon and best option. Thanks to God, I developed the courage to obey to this. It is so sweet to forgive; it gives you divine credit that only those who forgive can understand. You don't have to wait to forgive until after the one who offended you asked for it. The mere fact that you were offended, you are obliged to forgive, and this hits the devil into the face: Forgiving before you are asked demonstrates the character of Jesus in you. While He was still on the cross, he breathed out forgiveness in His last moments, saying, *"Father, forgive them; for they do not know what they are doing"*[102] It shows love and passion, which we should have when we are offended. Jesus did not wait for His resurrection to forgive but forgave when he was still bleeding and dirty on the cross; when a human being does this, it confuses the devil's mind.

Here is my advice to you who are holding this book: however dark the night may be, the morning will come. Everything humans do has an end. Nothing lasts forever except the word of God. Don't give up on your challenges. Don't listen to what laymen say. Listen to what God tells you and what His faithful servants say. People don't have the perfect answers for you when you are being challenged. Whatever solution man can give is temporary, but God has smooth and permanent solutions to obstacles. Stick to Him until things are going right. Do you have a church that will help you transform your life? If yes, good; now do what the Bible says. If not, please find one. Pursuing legal solutions might not be the best option for you and might not serve you right.

When I turn around, I see many people still in the "sinking boat" and out of compassion; I give you my words to strengthen you with principles that came out of personal experience. I understand what it is

---

Notes:

[101] T. D. Jakes, *Naked and Not Ashamed* (Shippensburg, PA: Treasure House, 2001)

[102] Luke 23:34NASB

like to be in a violent relationship and it is important to feel safe, after all, at some point God asked Joseph and Mary to seek refuge for baby Jesus when King Herod wanted him dead[103], but make sure that at secure places you can still come back and claim what is rightfully yours. Like I said that a home is a pitch where devil and God fight, some battles need fighters to meet face to face and tangle with the enemy while others need missiles. Carry out an assessment, evaluate your circumstances if you have Jesus as a comrade and commander in chief, better stay at it, He is not a baby any more but a super warrior and He likes being present at the battle fields, if you do not have Him, He can still be received but what is important is to ensure that you do not give up for the devil to steal your blessings. I cannot make you understand the joy of victory, but the bad times will be like a bad dream. We need to have guidance and Jesus does it better.

God bless you.

Notes:
[103] Mathew 2:13-23NASB

About the Author

Enid Muragira (full name Uwimana Enid Muragira Mutabaruka) has been married to Eric Mutabaruka since 1996 with whom they have four children. She is an experienced internal auditor, with a master's degree in audit management and consultancy from Birmingham City University, UK. She worked at Rwanda Revenue Authority for over fourteen years, and currently the Chief Audit Executive at the Central Bank of Rwanda.

Bibliography

The Bible
Fascinating Womanhood online class, 2009.